Michael Francis Pennock

THE SEEKER'S CATECHISM

The Basics of Catholicism

Presented in light of the new
Catechism of the Catholic Church

AVE MARIA PRESS   Notre Dame, Indiana 46556

Michael Francis Pennock has been a religious educator with adults and young adults for over twenty-five years. A graduate of Loyola University in Chicago, he holds a master's degree from St. John College in Cleveland and a Ph.D. from the University of Akron.

He is the author of *This Is Our Faith*, a comprehensive and widely praised catechism for adults, and the *Friendship in the Lord* series of high school religion texts.

Excerpts from THE NEW JERUSALEM BIBLE, copyright © 1985 by Darton, Longman & Todd, Ltd. and Doubleday & Company, Inc. Reprinted by permission of the publisher.

Nihil Obstat: Reverend Peter M. Mihalic, S.T.D., M.Div.
Censor Deputatus

Imprimatur: The Most Reverend Anthony M. Pilla, D.D.,
M.A., Bishop of Cleveland

Given at Cleveland, Ohio, on 15 April 1994.

The *Nihil Obstat* and *Imprimatur* are official declarations that a book or pamphlet is free of doctrinal or moral error. No implication is contained therein that those who have granted the *Nihil Obstat* and *Imprimatur* agree with the contents, opinions, or statements expressed.

English translation of the *Catechism of the Catholic Church* for the United States of America copyright ©1994, United States Catholic Conference, Inc. — Lireria Editrice Vaticana. Used with permission.

International Standard Book Number: 0-87793-539-4
Library of Congress Catalog Card Number: 94-71886

Cover design by Elizabeth J. French
Printed and bound in the United States of America

CONTENTS

Introduction

"Leave your country, your kindred and your father's house for a country which I shall show you; and I shall make you a great nation, I shall bless you and make your name famous; you are to be a blessing!"

—Genesis 12:1-2

These words of God addressed to Abraham propelled him on a journey of faith. Leaving his native land he set out with his wife Sarah, neither one of them knowing where their journey would lead them, but with faith in the promise that had been spoken. When they finally arrived in the land of Canaan, they found themselves to be "strangers in a strange land."

The faith of Abraham and Sarah did indeed give birth to a great nation, and we are recipients of their legacy. But like them, we are also "strangers in a strange land" who are on a lifelong journey which has as its ultimate destination union with the God who made us and sustains us.

I offer this book to those who want to know more about how the Catholic community journeys to the Father. In particular, I hope it will be useful for those who are discovering the role faith has in their own life journey for the first time. Perhaps you have recently come to inquire about the Catholic faith, or maybe you are returning to it after a long time away. You may indeed feel like a "stranger in a strange land," but hopefully this brief book will make you feel more at home with our beliefs and practices and encourage you to join us in our life of faith.

In light of the publication of the *Catechism of the Catholic Church*, I thought it was important to offer an exposition of faith that would incorporate the teachings of this important new text as well as other church statements issued in recent years. This book has its roots in *This Is Our Faith*, a longer summary of the Catholic faith I wrote in 1989. In an effort to provide a concise, more introductory book, I have selected key questions from *This Is Our Faith* and provided shorter responses based on that text. These have, in turn, been enriched by brief quotes from scripture, the *Catechism of the Catholic Church*, the documents of Vatican II, and recent encyclicals such as *The Splendor of Truth*. I would refer those who wish a fuller treatment of any of these questions to *This Is Our Faith*.

I invite you, the reader of this book, on a journey of understanding, of faith sharing, and of prayer and reflection on the Catholic faith. My own prayer for all of us is that we come to love our Lord Jesus Christ even more. Let us never forget that the teaching of and about the church has one major purpose: to draw us to Jesus.

1

THE EXISTENCE OF GOD

Every thinking, feeling human at some time has an awesome experience that shakes the very ground he or she walks on. At such times most of us turn to God, to wonder about that hidden presence which we have somehow sensed in our hearts. These experiences force us to ask questions about the meaning of life and death.

Does God exist?

St. Paul and the church assert that humans are rationally able to discover the hidden God because "ever since the creation of the world, the invisible existence of God and his everlasting power have been clearly seen by the mind's understanding of created things" (Rom 1:20). Belief in God is not unreasonable.

What does personal experience tell us about God?

Experience can guide us to God. Our feelings of dependency, our sense of wonder, awe and joy, our openness to truth and beauty, our feelings of being invited to do greater things than we are doing—all speak of a God who has made us to discover him. Here are the traditional arguments for God's existence.

An unquenchable thirst for happiness. Did a Creator make us with a hunger for happiness which nothing can completely satisfy? Might it be that God implanted in us a kind of homing device causing restlessness until we find him? This restlessness for *total* happiness points to a God who made us this way.

Sense of justice. We have a fundamental sense of moral goodness, a feeling that things will be reversed someday, that there is a Power that will right all wrongs, if not in this life, then in the next.

Love. Love is a spiritual reality that is not explained by materiality. It must come from somewhere, ultimately from Love itself, the being we call God.

What does human history tell us about God?

Human history is a powerful argument for the existence of God. There seems to be an intelligence behind our evolving history.

From the earliest times human beings have testified to the existence of God. An overwhelming majority of cultures have believed in some being who is greater than any of its members. We know *someone* is there, but God's true identity is not clear. We need divine help to know God as God really is.

What do demonstrations based on reason tell us about God?

St. Thomas Aquinas, the great medieval theologian, summed up five so-called proofs for the existence of God. A key proof is the logical conclusion that all creatures must ultimately come from a cause which itself was not caused. This "Uncaused Cause" is God. Besides philosophical arguments, our own personal reflection on creation's beauty, immensity, and power can give us an awareness of a God who made all things and keeps them in existence.

Does God communicate with us?

God not only exists, but he freely chose to communicate himself and the divine plan for salvation to us. The Second Vatican Council taught:

In His goodness and wisdom, God chose to reveal Himself and to make known to us the hidden purpose of His will by which through Christ, the Word made flesh, man has access to the Father in the Holy Spirit and comes to share in the divine nature (*Dogmatic Constitution on Divine Revelation*, No. 2).

What is divine revelation?

Christians believe God freely chose to communicate himself and the divine plan for salvation to us. God did this gradually by deeds and words inherently connected to each other. This free gift of God's self-communication is known as supernatural or divine revelation. God's self-disclosure and invitation to a deeper life of love are purely gifts on God's part.

At many moments in the past and by many means, God spoke to our ancestors through the prophets; but in our own time, the final days, he has spoken to us in the person of his Son, whom he appointed heir of all things and through whom he made the ages (Heb 1:1-2).

The story of God's self-disclosure, God's saving action in history, is known as *salvation history* which reached its high point in the coming of Jesus, the fullness of God's revelation. Jesus is the Word of God made flesh, the Son who lived among us, taught us in human words and deeds about his Father, and completed the Father's work of salvation.

What is the Bible's role in salvation history?

The story of salvation history lives on in the Bible and in the tradition of the Christian community. The Hebrew scriptures (Old Testament) record God's teaching to the Jewish people and God's interactions in their history. The New Testament chronicles the life and teachings of Jesus and announces the good news of God's plan of salvation for all people.

How does God help us respond to revelation?

We need to respond to God's self-communication and the revelation of God's plan for us. This response is known as *faith*. Faith, like revelation, is a free gift from God which gives conviction, commitment, and trust with regard to realities that we can neither see nor clearly prove.

Through this unearned gift of faith received at baptism, we join a community of believers in the Lord Jesus who lives in our midst. Faith, along with hope and love, make up the theological virtues.

- *Faith*, cooperating with divine grace, enables us to know God and believe what God reveals and the Catholic church proposes for our belief. Through faith we commit our whole person—intellect, will, actions, words—to the God who reveals.
- *Hope* empowers us to desire and trust firmly in God's loving salvation and that God will give us what we need to attain it.
- *Love* is God's own grace-filled life in us. It impels us to live Christ's life of caring concern and service for others.

2

GOD
Our Loving Creator

In the Creed we profess belief in one God, the Father, the Almighty, the Creator. The Bible reveals that the very nature of God is love. God asks us to love in return as the way to happiness.

What does God reveal?

A prime means of listening to God is by reading and reflecting on the Hebrew scriptures and the New Testament. Christians believe that these writings— the Bible—are God's words in human words:

> Through all the words of Sacred Scripture, God speaks only one single Word, his one utterance in whom he expresses himself completely (*Catechism of the Catholic Church [CCC]*, #102).

The Bible, which literally means "The Book," is a collection of books which contain different kinds of literature—poetry, history, religious myth (story), prayers, proverbs and the like. They have one thing in common though: All are *inspired* because God influenced the biblical writers in such a way that they recorded what God wanted. Inspiration refers to the guidance of the Holy Spirit in this writing process.

Catholics recognize forty-six books as the official list (*canon*) of inspired books of the Hebrew scriptures. What do these books reveal about God? The following points summarize some key truths about God.

There is only one God.

When God chose to reveal himself to humans, God began with the Israelites (Jews), the Chosen

People. Their history is one of *covenant*; that is, a solemn commitment. In return for God's great blessings and constant faithfulness, the Jews were to obey God's law as summarized in the Ten Commandments. The most important aspect of the Israelites' response was to worship Yahweh (a mysterious name meaning "I Am Who Am") and to testify to Yahweh as the one, true God, the source of all being, the one who keeps everything in existence. All other gods were false and thus powerless.

We cannot know God.

God is essentially a mystery. God is totally other than creation, above and beyond it. God is eternal, unique, infinite and all-powerful, unchanging, supremely holy, and utterly simple—a pure Spirit. Yet, God is also present to and joined with creation. For example, God formed and sustained the Chosen People, befriended prophets who spoke on God's behalf, and promised a Messiah.

God is the Creator.

God made all things out of nothing; creation is freely, generously, and wisely made to manifest and share God's glory. In the divine wisdom, God both sustains and rules the world. And God created humans in the divine image, able to think, choose, and love. Our human nature unites both the spiritual and material worlds. Created "male and female" in God's friendship, humans possess fundamental dignity.

> God created everything for man, but man in turn was created to serve and love God and to offer all creation back to him (*CCC*, #358).

Evil exists because of our sin.

Because God created free beings and not mere puppets, humans had the chance to either accept or reject God's love. Original sin is the unhappy story of Adam and Eve's rejection of God's love told in the book of Genesis.

Their sin brought about a disunity between God and us. Genesis also tells us that this fractured relationship resulted in a corresponding disharmony between nature and us, and our alienation from one another.

God is loving, faithful, and true.

The major theme of salvation history is God's loving faithfulness to his unfaithful creatures. God's love is manifested through deeds as well as words. God's deeds reflect a saving God, one who rescues the Israelites from the bondage of slavery in Egypt, one who sustains them in the desert, one who gives them a land and a king, one who keeps them alive in captivity, and one who returns them to their land.

The high point of God's loving concern is the promise to send a Messiah, a savior, who will restore humanity's proper relationship with God. In fulfillment of this promise God sent Jesus Christ, God's only Son.

If God knows all, how can we have free will?

God's knowledge does not force us to do anything. God gave us freedom and respects that freedom even if it leads us away from God's love.

If God is good, why is there evil?

God does not create evil; evil is the absence of good. Rather, God permits evil. Evil enters the picture when free, intelligent creatures turn from God's love. We also believe that some evil in the universe results from fallen angels (devils) at odds with their Creator.

3
JESUS
Lord and Messiah

For countless people Jesus Christ is the model of greatness. Jesus reveals that the way to greatness is to live a life serving others and loving them without condition. His life, death, and resurrection have brought about our eternal salvation.

"Who do you say I am?"

Jesus asked the apostles who people thought he was. Many of his contemporaries thought Jesus was a great prophet, or John the Baptist come back to life, or even the prophet Elijah. Peter answered in faith, "You are the Christ" (Mk 8:29), the correct answer which would change his life forever. Jesus asks us today, "Who do you say I am?"

Did Jesus really exist?

Few people today seriously doubt the historical existence of Jesus. Ancient Roman writers like Tacitus and Pliny the Younger, and the Jewish historian Josephus take his existence for granted. A careful analysis of the gospels and what they record as the words of Jesus reveal that he must have existed. The teachings of Jesus bear the stamp of a memorable individual who taught with unique insight and authority.

The gospels are best described as faith summaries which announce the good news of salvation. The authors, the four evangelists, are not primarily interested in all the historical details of Jesus' life on earth, but rather in the good deeds he performed, the words of salvation he taught, and the meaning of his passion, death, resurrection, and glorification.

When were the gospels written?

The different gospels were written over a period of about thirty-five years. Mark wrote around A.D. 65, Luke and Matthew between A.D. 75 and 85, and John in the last decade of the first century. Each evangelist adapted his materials keeping in mind the circumstances of his particular audience.

What do we know about Jesus' early life?

Matthew and Luke write that Jesus was born of the virgin Mary in Bethlehem. Luke records that Jesus accompanied Mary and Joseph to Jerusalem for the great religious feasts of the Jews. Luke also writes that the twelve-year-old Jesus astounded the Temple teachers with his intelligence.

When did his public ministry begin?

Jesus next appears on the scene in the "fifteenth year of Tiberius Caesar's reign" (from A.D. 27-28) when he was in his thirties. He then launched his public ministry after being baptized by John the Baptist.

What qualities of Jesus do the gospels reveal?

He was a healer. He cured not only friends, but also lepers, the blind, the deaf, epileptics, the crippled, the possessed, and many others with various afflictions. Jesus demonstrated God's love in concrete actions on behalf of his people and that love has the power to overcome evil.

He was compassionate. The poor, the sinners, the abandoned, widows and children—all flocked to receive his love and understanding. He gave them what they really needed: the healing touch of God's forgiveness and the good news that they were loved.

He was courageous. He stood up to the false teachers of his day. He boldly preached the Father's will, knowing it would lead to his death.

He was humble. He was poor and owned no possessions. He came from a place that was ridiculed even by his disciples.

He was self-giving. His love, his concern for all people, his miracles, his message of God's forgiveness, his preaching about God's kingdom—all of this got him in trouble with the religious and political leaders of his time who plotted his death. Jesus freely gave his life for all people everywhere.

Did Jesus have brothers and sisters?

Catholics have traditionally believed that Jesus did not have physical brothers and sisters and that Mary was always a virgin. These beliefs are based on both the Bible and tradition. The gospels state that Mary was a virgin and that Jesus was conceived miraculously by the power of the Holy Spirit (Mt 1:20 and Lk 1:34). Church tradition has always taught the perpetual virginity of Mary. The texts in the gospels which refer to Jesus' brothers (and sisters) use a word which can also mean cousin or even some distant relations of the same generation.

What do titles reveal about Jesus?

Christ. "Christ" is one of the most important titles given to Jesus. It is the Greek word for the Hebrew title *Messiah,* meaning the "anointed one of Yahweh."

Suffering Servant. Jesus took on the burdens of his people and redeemed them.

Son of God. Through his work and words, Jesus revealed himself to be the unique Son of God.

Lord. The Hebrew scriptures used Lord for God alone. When Christians use this title for Jesus, they proclaim their belief that in him God is present and at work.

Son of Man. Jesus used this title for himself more than any other. It refers to Jesus as a human being and describes his role as the judge and the savior through whom God's reign will be established.

Word of God. Human words reveal our thoughts and symbolically express what is hidden. In a similar way, the Word of God (Jesus) perfectly reveals God the Father. The doctrine of the *incarnation* holds that the Word became flesh in Jesus. It is the mystery of the union of Christ's divine and human natures.

Belief in the true Incarnation of the Son of God is the distinctive sign of Christian faith (CCC, #463).

How was the apostolic faith preserved?

The first few centuries of the church's history were marked by its growth and its understanding of Jesus and the meaning of the paschal mystery. The church fathers—leading church thinkers and writers—preserved the apostolic faith in Jesus as they explained his message to people of their day.

What is a heresy?

During the first five centuries or so of Christianity, a number of false teachings, called heresies, about Jesus arose in the church. They clustered into two main categories: one that denied Jesus' humanity, the other that denied his divinity.

How was heresy dealt with?

The bishops called a series of ecumenical (worldwide) councils to carefully define the nature of

Jesus Christ. The teachings of these councils state the classic dogmas of Catholics and other Christians about Jesus Christ.

What did these councils teach?

These major ecumenical councils taught that:

● Jesus is true God. There was never a time when he was not God.

● There is only one person in Christ, the divine person, the Word of God, the second person of the Blessed Trinity. Thus, everything in Christ's human nature is to be attributed to his divine person, for example, his miracles and even his suffering and death.

● Mary, by conceiving God's Son, is truly the Mother of God.

● Jesus has a divine nature and a human nature. He is perfect in divinity and perfect in humanity.

● Jesus has a human intellect and a human will. Both are perfectly attuned and subject to his divine intellect and will, which he has in common with the Father and the Holy Spirit.

● As a true human being, body and soul, Jesus embodies the divine ways of God in a human way.

● The union of the human and divine natures in the one person of Jesus is so perfect that we say, in Jesus, God truly shared our life with us.

● Jesus, God-made-human, is our Savior. By uniting ourselves to his death and resurrection through faith, we will share in the eternal life he has won for us.

● Jesus will come in all his glory at the end of time to judge the living and the dead.

4

JESUS
Teacher and Savior

Jesus met and touched people. His touch always demanded some kind of response. The Lord continues to touch us today—through his church, in his holy word, in the sacraments, through other people. He continues to teach us. What he wants from us is change, conversion.

How did Jesus teach?

The Jesus of history was both a healer and a teacher. Jesus' teaching style was imaginative and provoked much interest. His whole life, every action and word he spoke, was his teaching. People were especially delighted with his parables—short stories with a religious message.

Does Jesus' teaching have meaning for today?

Christians believe that Jesus taught the most important message God ever delivered to us: the good news of salvation, the message that saves us and wins for us eternal life.

The gospels proclaim the meaning of the life, suffering, death, resurrection, and glorification of Jesus. But they also record the words of the Word of God. They show us the way to true happiness; they unlock the meaning of life.

What did Jesus teach?

What follows is a short summary of some of the major points of Jesus' teaching.

God's kingdom is already here. The term *kingdom of God* (or *reign of God*) refers to God's active concern for us. It means that God's will is being done on earth as it is in heaven. It means that God's justice, peace, and love are helping to unite God's children here on earth. Jesus himself ushers in the kingdom. His healing of people's physical, emotional, and spiritual hurts is a sign of the kingdom. Although the kingdom starts small and will meet resistance, it will inevitably grow and powerfully transform all humanity.

God is a loving Father. Jesus teaches that God is a loving Father. God's love is tender and beyond anything we can comprehend. We can approach God with total confidence because God will provide for us and meet our most pressing needs.

God is merciful. Jesus proclaims that God forgives all sin. Because God is so forgiving, we should be joyful, happy people and imitate the Father by forgiving those who have hurt us.

God's love is for everyone. God's kingdom is open to all. It is a free gift; we cannot earn it. We show our appreciation when we love others. Jesus taught that the love of God and neighbor are one. And who is our neighbor? Everyone, even our enemy.

Repentance and imitation of Jesus. If we want to enter the kingdom, we must turn from our sins and put on the mind of Jesus Christ. We must believe that Jesus is God's Son, the way to happiness, and become his disciples. We must be light to the world, allowing the Lord to shine through us by living lives of service. What we do to others, especially the "least of these," we do to the Lord.

The Lord is with us. Jesus promises that he will be with us until the end of time. He has sent us the Holy Spirit who unites us in love to the Father and the Son and to all our brothers and sisters. The Spirit—the living God who dwells within us—guides us, strengthens us, and sanctifies us as we try to follow in the Lord's footsteps.

To accept Jesus is to accept the cross. To follow Jesus into the kingdom means to do the will of God. Doing God's will involves self-denial and sacrifice. But Jesus promises that we will share in the peace and joy of the resurrection. A life of service means dying to selfishness, but leads to an eternal life of happiness.

Why do we call Jesus our savior?

Christians hold that Jesus Christ is the fullness of God's revelation. Everything that Jesus said and did revealed God. The words he spoke were from the Father, living in him, doing his work. He came to bring salvation. The very name *Jesus* means "God saves," thus expressing our Lord's identity *and* mission.

What is salvation?

Salvation refers to the good and happiness that God intends for us. It is the mending of broken relationships which keep us from being whole and at one with God and with our neighbor. It is the showering of God's blessings and the forgiveness of our sins.

What is the meaning of the passion and death of Jesus?

The teaching and life of Jesus is summed up in his passion and death on a cross. Jesus totally identified with the sufferings of all humans. He freely allowed himself to suffer and be put to death for the forgiveness of sins. His fidelity to his Father's will led him to a life of total service, of giving up everything he had for us—his very life.

The death of Jesus would be a tragic ending to the gospels except for the unparalleled fact of his resurrection. Through the death and resurrection of Jesus Christ, death itself died. The consequence of his incredible love for us was that he surrendered his life for our sakes. But the Father accepted his life as a gift on behalf of all of us and restored him to a superabundant, glorious, resurrected life.

What is the meaning of the resurrection?

Jesus is risen! The Lord appeared to his close followers and with his Father sent them the Holy Spirit to go out and continue his good work and to preach the forgiveness of sin and the good news that sin and death have been conquered. Jesus' resurrection confirms his teachings, life, and promises; underscores his divinity; opens a new life for us; brings about our adoption into God's family; and is the basis for our own future resurrection.

What is the paschal mystery?

The paschal mystery refers to Jesus' passion, death, resurrection, and glorification. Through these key events of our salvation, Jesus redeemed us from slavery to sin. He shares his life with us and through the Holy Spirit instructs us that love of God and neighbor is the vocation of all who belong to God's family.

5

THE HOLY SPIRIT
The Power of Love

Christians believe in the active presence of the Holy Spirit whose life-giving friendship works for us until the end of time. The Spirit transforms our lives from within. The Spirit's gifts enable us to accomplish God's saving work for others and the world in which we live. The Spirit is the mystery of God's love alive in the world.

What does spirit mean?

A common philosophical definition describes *spirit* as "the life force of living beings." Without spirit, there is no enthusiasm, no life.

What does spirit mean in a religious sense?

Christians refer to God as spirit. We believe that the Holy Spirit is the third person of the Blessed Trinity, the Spirit of the Father with whom Jesus is filled. The Holy Spirit is the Father and Son's love, a gift to all of Jesus' followers.

What does the New Testament say about the Holy Spirit?

The Acts of the Apostles and St. Paul's letters make many references to the Holy Spirit. The gospels also contain important references. John the Baptist is filled with the Spirit in his mother's womb. His parents, Elizabeth and Zachary, are also filled with the Spirit. The Spirit overshadows the virgin Mary at the time of the Lord's conception and is present at his baptism, during the time of his desert temptations, throughout his teaching and healing ministries, and during his passion and death. Jesus also taught about the Spirit, for example, to Nicodemus (Jn 3:5-8) and to the Samaritan woman (Jn 4:10, 14, 23-24). Finally, it was through the Spirit that the Father raised Jesus from the dead.

The Holy Spirit is the very presence of the risen, glorified Lord, the Spirit of Love who exists with the Father and Son from all eternity. The Holy Spirit helps Christians on the great mission of continuing Jesus' work of forgiveness and reconciliation.

The gift of the Holy Spirit enabled the apostles, and enables us, to know and to love Jesus in a new way.

How does the Spirit appear in the Hebrew scriptures?

The writers of the Hebrew scriptures also refer to the *Spirit* of God, but for them it has the meaning "wind" and "breath"—the breath that gives life. They also describe the Spirit of Yahweh in personal terms—guiding, instructing, causing people to rest. They treat God's Spirit as action rather than person. God's Spirit (wind) creates the earth by sweeping over the watery void (Gn 1:1-2); God creates humans by breathing his Spirit into their nostrils (Gn 2:7). The Spirit also enables the prophets to speak on God's behalf. The Hebrew scriptures tell us that God's Spirit will help God's people keep the law and that it will be poured out on all people when the Messiah comes.

What are some images of the Spirit?

In Christian art the Holy Spirit is most often depicted as a dove—a symbol of peace, innocence, and God's mysterious presence. The Bible uses other images— among them wind, fire, tongues of fire, and water—when it speaks of the Spirit's mysterious but real presence.

Wind. A driving wind signalled the advent of the Holy Spirit at Pentecost. Genesis also speaks of God's Spirit hovering over the watery chaos at the time of the creation of the world. Wind is a powerful image— something invisible but with quite evident effects. The image of Spirit as wind underscores the life and freedom given God's people through the Holy Spirit.

Fire. Fire evokes images of light, warmth, transformation, power, mystery. The Hebrew scriptures refer to God as a consuming fire, even appearing to Moses in a burning bush. Pillars of fire guided the Israelites through the desert at night and symbolized Yahweh's judgment on the Chosen People. It purified the holy and destroyed the wicked.

Jesus refers to himself as the light of the world and calls on his disciples to be light as well. The Spirit is the inner light who gives us the capacity to know and love Jesus.

Tongues of Fire. The tongue is an organ of speech. Filled with the Holy Spirit, Jesus spoke for God; his words were the Father's words. When tongues of fire descended on the apostles, they were given the power to preach the truth about Jesus. And they were understood, even by people who did not speak their language. The Holy Spirit unifies, breaking down the barriers between individuals and among the people and God.

Water. Genesis reminds us of two important functions of water: destruction and life. God created out of the watery chaos and when people sinned, God punished them with the flood. And Yahweh led the Chosen People to springs of water in the desert. In baptism, water symbolizes death to a life of sin and a rebirth to an eternal life. Baptism represents initiation into the Body of Christ and bestows the gift of the Holy Spirit.

What is grace?

Grace is the gift of the Holy Spirit that makes us children of God and brothers and sisters to one another. Grace is a share in God's own life.

Sanctifying grace is the gift of divine life in us who have been made holy by rebirth in baptism and union with the Holy Spirit. It enables us to participate in God's own life and become the "image and likeness" of God that God calls us to be.

Actual grace is God's help to do good and avoid evil in the concrete circumstances of our lives. The Holy Spirit living in us calls us to act as God's children and helps us live a Spirit-filled life.

What are the gifts of the Spirit?

The Holy Spirit showers us with many gifts to accomplish God's work. The Spirit teaches us to pray and grants us the seven gifts needed for a Christian life: *wisdom, understanding, right judgment, courage, knowledge, reverence,* and *wonder and awe in God's presence.* The Spirit gives each of us special gifts needed to build up the Lord's body. Some of us are called to be prophets; others to proclaim the good news; some to heal; others to minister and teach.

What are the fruits of the Spirit?

The Holy Spirit makes us Christlike, makes us holy. The Spirit is the source of the good that we see in those who are alive in Christ. The fruits of the Holy Spirit—*love, joy, peace, patient endurance, kindness, generosity, faith, mildness,* and *chastity*—are the signs and sources of our happiness.

How do we experience the Spirit today?

We experience the Holy Spirit in the church, the Body of Christ. The Spirit speaks to us through the Bible, in tradition, and in the church's teaching authority—the magisterium—which guides us in living Christlike lives. We also experience the Holy Spirit in the words and symbols of the sacraments, in prayer, in the gifts and ministries which build up the church, in the signs of apostolic and missionary life, and in the witness of the saints.

The mission of Christ and the Holy Spirit is brought to completion in the Church, which is the Body of Christ and the Temple of the Holy Spirit (CCC, #737).

6

THE BLESSED TRINITY
Unity in Community

Christians believe that God is self-revealed to us as a trinity of persons—the Father, the Son, and the Holy Spirit. The Blessed Trinity is the central doctrine of Catholic faith from which other teachings are derived.

Who is God?

When Moses asked God for his name, God responded, "Yahweh," which means "I am who am." This means, simply, Yahweh is *being* itself. Yahweh is truth.

What does Jesus teach us of God the Father?

Jesus addresses God as *Abba*, a simple term of endearment. Jesus tells the apostles that they—and we—can address God as *Abba*, too. Jesus taught us that the Father loves us in a way that is beyond our comprehension. The Father loves immeasurably and unconditionally. We can't earn this love; it is a gift showered on good and evil people alike.

Our loving Father will take care of all our needs. God knows our needs and will give us what is good for us. St. Paul reminds us that the Father creates all things and wills the salvation of everyone through his Son.

The idea of God as Mother also adds to our understanding of God's love for us. A good mother tenderly protects, unblinkingly forgives, and unconditionally accepts her child. Every child who experiences true motherly love knows that it is the most natural, available, compassionate, and serving kind of love known to us. God's love is exactly like that.

Thinking about God as Mother or Father is helpful, but we must remember that God is neither male nor female. God embodies all the positive qualities we associate with both fathers and mothers— creativity, sustenance, nurture, guidance, availability, and love. But God possesses them without limit. God's love is unimaginably greater than the love of any human father or mother.

What do we know of God the Son?

Christians believe that Jesus is "the human face of God." Jesus called God Father and related to him in a unique way. He taught that only the Son knows the Father, that all the Father has is his, that the Father has given him all power, and that his words are the words of the Father who sent him. If we know Jesus, we know the Father.

Everything about Jesus reveals the Father. His presence, his words, his healing touches, his forgiving glances, and especially his death and resurrection show us what is really real. They reveal God because Jesus is the Word of God.

What do we know of God the Holy Spirit?

The Spirit empowered the early Christians on Pentecost Sunday and was with the Lord throughout his ministry. Moreover, Jesus promised to send the Paraclete to his followers. He promised that the Spirit of truth and love would take up his dwelling in God's people.

The Holy Spirit attracts us to the Son so that we are able to recognize him as the Messiah, our Savior. The Spirit enables us to proclaim that God is our Father. And the Spirit is the source of all good gifts given us by our gracious, loving God.

The mystery of the Most Holy Trinity is the central mystery of Christian faith and life. It is the mystery of God in himself. It is therefore the source of all other mysteries of faith, the light that enlightens them, and the most fundamental and essential teaching in the "hierarchy of the truths of the faith" (CCC, #234).

How does the Trinity relate to us?

We can never fully comprehend the doctrine of the Trinity. God is beyond full human knowledge. God is more intimate to us than we are to ourselves. God chose to approach us through Jesus and take up his dwelling in us through the Holy Spirit. This is the mystery of love itself: We have been given a glimpse of God's own life.

God the Father creates all things and continues to give life and being to everything in creation. God the Son lived among us, taught us of the Father's love, and won for us eternal salvation. God the Holy Spirit is the Love of God who dwells in us and in the church. The Spirit is the source of unity, courage, truth, and love for all humanity.

What are the relationships within the Trinity?

Another way to approach the mystery of the Trinity is to reflect on God as three persons: Father, Son, and Holy Spirit. But we must not think of *person* in the same sense as we are persons. There are not three separate consciousnesses in God. There is only one simple being. There are not three separate intelligences or wills in the one God. When one person of the Trinity acts, the other two persons also act. Each person is *distinct* but does not act separately from the others. God is one, a community in unity.

God acts as one, though we *appropriate* or attribute certain actions to each of the persons; for example, *creation* to the Father, *redemption* to the Son, and *sanctification* to the Holy Spirit.

Traditional Catholic teaching explains the relationships among the three persons of the Trinity this way:

The Father. The first person of the Trinity is absolutely without origin. From all eternity he "begets" the Son, the second person of the Trinity.

The Son. The Son is the Father's perfect, divine expression of himself, the Word of God. They are one, yet distinct.

The Holy Spirit. The Father and Son love each other with an eternal, perfect, divine love. The love *proceeds* from the Father and the Son and is called the third person of the Trinity, the Holy Spirit. The Holy Spirit is the Spirit of Love between the Father and the Son; the Spirit binds them into a community of unity.

7

THE CHRISTIAN COMMUNITY

The church, a community founded by Jesus Christ, shares common interests and works for common goals. It's a family of believers formed in Jesus' name and sustained by the Holy Spirit.

Christians are quite diverse and individually unique. But they do have something vital in common: By virtue of their baptism into the Christian family, they come together as a community to acknowledge and celebrate the Lordship of Jesus Christ.

The Lord brings us together and unites us into his people in order to continue his work on earth. We are united in that work with our Christian brothers and sisters who have gone before us in death and with those who will come after us.

What is the church?

The church is the community of those who acknowledge Jesus as Lord; it is a community of believers who live a sacramental life and who commit themselves to fellowship and service for the sake of God's reign. Above all else it is the mystery of God's loving grace.

Because the church is unlike any other human community, no one definition or description can exhaust its rich meaning. The Second Vatican Council used biblical images to describe the church: mystery, the People of God, the Body of Christ, the sacrament of Jesus.

The Bible alludes to many other images of the church, for example, pilgrim, God's building and farm, Christ's bride, the heavenly Jerusalem, and the flock of Christ.

What does the church as "mystery" mean?

St. Augustine defined a *mystery* as a visible sign of some invisible grace. To call the church a mystery is to say that the invisible, almighty God is working through this faith community, this institution which exists to continue the saving work of Jesus Christ.

St. Paul calls the nuptial union of Christ and the Church "a great mystery." Because she is united to Christ as to her bridegroom, she becomes a mystery in her turn (*CCC*, #772).

What does the church as "People of God" mean?

The image of the church as the People of God has its roots in the Old Testament covenant between God and Israel by which God wished to sanctify and save not only individuals but individuals formed into a loving community. This image emphasizes the dignity of each Christian, a temple of the Holy Spirit called into a fellowship of life, love, and truth.

The People of God are those of us who are baptized and acknowledge that Jesus Christ is Lord and Savior. Our mission is to live our lives in such a way that the Lord's light shines forth in the world through us. When we love, God's love can be seen.

Is the church the same as God's reign?

God's reign, his saving activity in human history which draws all people to him, is different from the church. The church includes only baptized members. The reign of God extends to all people who are saved for all time. But the church and the reign of God are intimately connected.

The church is the initial budding of the reign of God; its members work on its behalf in an explicit, conscious way. The full flowering of this reign will take place at the end of human history.

What does the church as "Body of Christ" mean?

This important image of the church can be traced to St. Paul who wrote:

Now Christ's body is yourselves, each of you with a part to play in the whole (1 Cor 12:27).

The risen, glorified Lord is present in the world today through Christians. We are his hands, his loving touch, his understanding glance, his sympathetic word of comfort to the lonely and suffering, his instrument used to preach the good news of salvation.

Christ is the head of the body, we are its members. We become incorporated into the body through baptism. The Holy Spirit unites the members into one body.

The church as the Body of Christ also underscores the dignity of each individual member. Just as each member of a person's body has a specific and important function to play, so, too, in the church each member has a specific and important role to play.

The Church is the Bride of Christ; he loved her and handed himself over for her. He has purified her by his blood and made her the fruitful mother of all God's children (CCC, #808).

The Church is the Temple of the Holy Spirit. The Spirit is the soul, as it were, of the Mystical Body, the source of its life, of its unity in diversity, and of the riches of its gifts and charisms (CCC, #809).

Is the church perfect?

When Christians love, they build up the Body of Christ. Because the church includes a human, as well as a divine dimension, the church can sin. The story of the Christian people reveals that we are both holy and sinful. We are a pilgrim people, a people on our way to total union with God. We are not yet perfect.

What does the church as "sacrament of Jesus" mean?

A sacrament is a special kind of sign or symbol. A symbol, by definition, is something concrete that points to another reality. A sacrament is also an *efficacious symbol*. That means it brings about what it points to; it embodies the very reality that it represents. Thus it is accurate to say that Jesus is the sacrament of God's love. Jesus not only points to God; he is God. He not only symbolizes God's love; he is God's love. He is what he represents.

The church is a concrete sign of Christ's presence to all people. It is an outward, visible sign of God's loving gift of himself in human history. Like other efficacious symbols, the church must point to something. It must lead us to Christ who is united to people through the church. The church helps put us in touch with the Lord whom it represents.

How does the church lead us to Christ?

The church is a sacrament of Christ when it presents the *message* of God's love in Jesus Christ, builds up the Christian *community*, *serves* all people, especially those in need, and *worships* God the Father through Jesus Christ in the Holy Spirit.

Message. Down through the centuries the church has announced the good news that the God of love invites all people to the fullness of life. The church must continue to preach this message to all people everywhere.

Community. To be an effective and credible sign of the gospel, others must be able to see in the church a community united by faith, hope, and love. If non-believers see loving, caring people, they naturally take notice and ask themselves what this group stands for.

Service. The third task of the church is service. Jesus showed us the way when he took off his cloak and washed the apostles' feet at the Last Supper. A Christian should serve, should minister to the needs of others. The church must witness to God's love by translating its words of love into concrete acts of service for all.

Worship. Entrusted to the church are the means of sanctification, especially the sacred mysteries—the sacraments. The celebration of the eucharist is a special moment in the life of the church because it celebrates and creates Christian community. It enables members of the church to become Christ for others.

8

THE CHURCH
Its Mission and Nature

Message, community, service, and worship summarize our Christ-given mission. This is why the Lord wants each individual member of his body to herald the gospel, build Christian community, serve others, and worship God. Another way of looking at our mission is through the roles of prophet, priest, and king. The church as a whole has the duty to continue the prophetic, priestly, and kingly roles assumed by Jesus himself. Individual Christians have a prophetic, priestly, and kingly function.

How does the church function as prophet?

A prophet is someone who speaks the word of God. All church members share in the prophetic mission of Jesus. Because we are baptized, Jesus asks us to witness to his truth in words and actions.

Lay people also fulfill their prophetic mission by evangelization, "that is, the proclamation of Christ by word and testimony of life" (CCC, #905).

What is the church's role as prophet?

The institutional church is also empowered by this gift of prophecy. Jesus entrusted to his church the task of authentically and truthfully proclaiming the word as it appears in scripture and tradition.

The church has been led through the centuries by the Holy Spirit. The Spirit helps the church authentically recognize and hand on what is essential to the Christian life. The pope, bishops, and pastors continue the ministry of Peter and the apostles who were singled out by the Lord during his historical lifetime to continue his work on earth. An organized leadership helps preserve authentic tradition and helps in the spreading of the true gospel.

Catholics believe that the pope is the successor of Peter. At the head of the bishops—the successors of the apostles—the pope has primacy over the whole church. The pope and the bishops form a single entity called the college of bishops. The bishops in communion with one another and with the pope must teach truthfully the word of God. The pope's special role is to be a sign of unity when the bishops speak as one. He speaks with the bishops as the voice of Jesus Christ alive in the church.

How does the church teach?

Normally the pope and bishops teach through the ordinary magisterium of the church. *Magisterium* refers to the office of teaching in the church which the Lord gave to the apostles and their successors. All Catholics recognize the right of the pope, bishops, pastors, and priests to teach on behalf of the Lord Jesus.

The mission of the Magisterium is linked to the definitive nature of the covenant established by God with his people in Christ. It is this Magisterium's task to preserve God's people from deviations and defections and to guarantee them the objective possibility of professing the true faith without error (*CCC*, #890).

What is infallibility?

Based on our Lord's promise that the church could not go astray because of his continuous presence, Catholics believe that on essential matters of faith and morals, the church is *infallible*. This is the belief that a certain doctrine (teaching) is free of error.

What is papal infallibility?

The pope speaks infallibly when he teaches under the following conditions:

- as the visible head of the whole church,
- to all Catholics,
- on a matter of faith or morals,
- intending to use his full authority in an unchangeable decision.

This kind of teaching is rare. Only once in the last one hundred years has the pope proclaimed an infallible teaching: the doctrine of the assumption of Mary into heaven in 1950 by Pope Pius XII.

Papal infallibility refers solely to the pope's power or gift as successor of Peter to teach correctly Christ's revelation, especially when it is attacked or denied thus leading to confusion among God's people. The pope's personal opinions and beliefs, like any person's, can be wrong, for example, in politics, science, or sports. In addition, because the pope is human, he can sin and make mistakes, even in the way he governs the church. Like all gifts of the Holy Spirit, infallibility is meant to build up the Body of Christ and give us access to the truth of Christ.

What is the church's role as priest?

The church's primary role is to lead directly to the sanctification of others. A priest is someone who helps to bring others to Christ. All Christians share in the common priesthood of Jesus in many different ways. Some are called to act as official teachers, others to preside at the eucharistic sacrifice and to forgive sins in our Lord's name. Though only some are called to be ordained, everyone in the church—clergy and laity alike—has the baptismal call to holiness. The measure of our personal greatness in God's eyes is not our special gifts, but rather the intensity of love we have for God and others.

What do we mean by the church as king?

When we think of a king, we think of a ruler, an authority figure. Jesus reminds us that all authority resides in him. The Lord has chosen to share his authority with shepherds in the church. He shares his teaching authority in a special way with the pope, bishops, and pastors. He also shares his ruling authority. The office of ruling in the church has but one purpose: the growth of faith and holiness.

The church's ruling must be done with humility, love, and compassion. The church's standards must be those of Christ, never the standards of worldly rulers. The model of church as king must be that of a serving king. As a constant reminder of this truth, Pope John Paul II has taken the motto: The servant of the servants of God.

What is the nature of the church?

Traditionally the church has been known by four signs or marks which help identify its true nature: one, holy, catholic, and apostolic. These marks help to strengthen the faith of Catholics.

But the signs are paradoxical in nature. They refer to the divine element—Christ and the Holy Spirit—working in the church. And yet the church is made up of human members who sometimes betray the very marks which should point to the Lord. These marks need some explanation.

How is the church one?

The church's unity is rooted in the unity of the Blessed Trinity. There are three different kinds of unity in the Roman Catholic Church.

Unity of Creed. A creed is a body of beliefs. The creed is officially taught by the magisterium of the church, and all Catholics are united in their belief.

Unity of Moral Teaching. The code of the church refers to the moral teachings of the church and their application to concrete contemporary issues. Catholics are united in the church's ongoing quest to discover God's will in the solution of moral problems.

Unity of Worship. The sacred liturgy—the Mass, the other sacraments, and the Liturgy of the Hours—is celebrated around the world and has been a source of unity for Catholic worship down through the centuries.

Unity does not necessarily mean *uniformity.* Even though Catholics from around the world worship the same way, there is room for local custom.

How is the church holy?

God is the ultimate source of holiness in the church and Jesus Christ, the founder of the church, is the model of holiness in the church. In a sense, only God is holy, but because the Holy Spirit lives in the church we can call the church holy. We may also say the church is holy because in it can be found "the fullness of the means of salvation," the means to the wholeness of personal development.

The church possesses in a unique way the means necessary to achieve this full personhood: the word of God which is found in the Bible, in apostolic tradition, in the writings of great saints and theologians, and in the teaching office of the church; the liturgical life of the church which includes the sacraments and most especially the holy eucharist; and in the various kinds of prayer practiced by Catholics through the centuries.

How is the church catholic?

The word *catholic* means "universal." The church is universal because Christ is in it. As St. Ignatius of Antioch observed, "Where there is Jesus Christ, there is the Catholic church." The church's universality manifests itself in three ways. First, by following the Lord's command to teach all nations, the church has reached out to all men and women at all times in all places. Second, the church is catholic in the sense that it continues to teach all that Christ taught. Finally, catholic refers to fullness—a Catholic has access to the fullness of a faith relationship in Jesus Christ.

How is the church apostolic?

The present leadership of the Catholic church can trace itself back to the first leaders of the church, the apostles. The bishops—successors to the apostles—in union with the pope continue to teach, sanctify, and guide the church until Christ comes again. The church is also apostolic in the sense that it professes the same doctrine and Christian way of life taught by the apostles. It has preserved the good news of Jesus and his salvation and has not changed anything essential in his preaching or that of his closest disciples.

Can non-Christians be saved?

Traditionally Catholics have taught that the church is necessary for salvation. Jesus himself taught the need for faith and baptism. Consequently, the church teaches that anyone, knowing "that the Catholic Church was made necessary by God through Jesus Christ, [who] would refuse to enter her or to remain in her could not be saved" (*Constitution on the Church*, #14).

What about those who have never heard of Jesus Christ? Can they be saved? The church answers yes. God's reign includes those who are mysteriously drawn to it through the workings of the Holy Spirit in their lives. Their vocation is to seek the kingdom of God as they know it, and live as lovingly as they possibly can.

9

CATHOLIC MORALITY
Living the Christian Life

Our key Catholic beliefs center on faith in Jesus Christ as Lord and Savior. But Christianity is more than a set of beliefs; it is a way of living. Christian faith must result in a life of loving service or it is an empty faith. Christian morality helps us discover how we should live our lives as a result of our faith in God's word which has been revealed to us.

What is Christian morality?

Christian morality can be summarized in the word *responsibility*. There are two components to this term: *response* and *ability*. To what do we respond? Christian life is a response to God's freely given love and his gift of salvation offered to us through Jesus Christ. "Following Christ is thus the essential and primordial foundation of Christian morality" (Pope John Paul II, *The Splendor of Truth*, #19). Christian morality comes to the forefront when people say yes to God, when they freely respond to his love. The essence of Christian morality is, simply, love. Reflect on the words of Jesus:

> *"You must love the Lord your God with all your heart, with all your soul*, and with all your mind. This is the greatest and the first commandment. The second resembles it: *You must love your neighbor as yourself"* (Mt 22:37-39).

The second aspect of Christian morality is the ability to respond to God, the ability to love, the ability to say yes to God. This is also a gift, also freely bestowed on us. It is part of what it means to be a human being. Human persons have basic dignity which flows from their being created in God's image (with a soul); this implies that we can think and love and are in relationship to others in community. Our conscience aids us in a life directed to God and other people.

What is a covenant?

When we reflect on the Christian life as a response to God's invitation to life and to love, we are stressing the *covenant* relationship between God and his children.

A covenant is the strongest possible pledge between two parties, typically of unequal rank, wherein certain commitments are made. The Hebrew scriptures reveal Yahweh as a God who entered into a number of covenants with humans in general and the Jews in particular. In these covenants, Yahweh was always faithful. In return, God wanted God's people to be faithful to the covenant. For the Chosen People this meant that living the Law was a way to *respond* to God. The Law, summarized in the Ten Commandments, was not seen as a list of burdensome obligations to be tolerated, but as a way to live out the special identity bestowed on the Jewish people.

What is the New Testament covenant?

The most important covenant of all is the covenant of love God has made with all people through his Son Jesus. The New Testament covenant is a new pledge in Christ's blood. Jesus' death and resurrection seal our relationship with the Father. Christians respond to their vocation as children of God in two ways: first, by living the Ten Commandments and second, by trying to live the Sermon on the Mount as summarized in the Beatitudes.

Christian morality consists ... in *following Jesus Christ,* in abandoning oneself to him, in letting oneself be transformed by his grace and renewed by his mercy, gifts which come to us in the living communion of his Church. ... The one who loves Christ keeps his commandments (cf. Jn 14:15) (*The Splendor of Truth,* #119).

What are the Ten Commandments?

The Ten Commandments are found in Exodus 20:2-17 and Deuteronomy 5:6-21. The summary below is from the *New American Bible* translation.

1. I, the Lord, am your God. You shall not have other gods besides me.

2. You shall not take the name of the Lord, your God, in vain.

3. Remember to keep holy the sabbath day.

4. Honor your father and your mother.

5. You shall not kill.

6. You shall not commit adultery.

7. You shall not steal.

8. You shall not bear false witness against your neighbor.

9. You shall not covet your neighbor's wife.

10. You shall not covet anything that belongs to your neighbor.

"Love God Above All Things"
(The First Three Commandments)

I, the Lord, am your God. You shall not have other gods besides me. The first commandment sets the priority for the Christian life. Simply put, friendship with God which leads to eternal union with God must be the ultimate goal of our lives. There is always the temptation to make something else the be-all and

end-all of our existence. Sex, money, power, possessions, and prestige are all good in their place, but
when we end up worshipping them, we have failed
to recognize the one who created them; thus, we are
unfaithful.

We honor the first commandment when we
gratefully acknowledge, worship, and thank the
source of everything in existence—God, our loving
Creator. The first commandment calls us to believe
and hope in God and love God above everything.

The first commandment forbids any form of
idolatry, superstition, astrology, divination, or
spiritism.

*You shall not take the name of the Lord, your God, in
vain.* The second commandment stresses our need to
respect the Lord's name and to practice our religion
humbly. The Christian realizes that what we say
reflects who we are. Some things are sacred, including God's name, and our language and attitude to our
religion should be respectful. Thus, cursing—asking
God to harm another—is wrong. Blasphemy—
abusive or disrespectful remarks made against
God—and swearing oaths falsely using God's name
are also against the values of the second commandment.

Remember to keep holy the sabbath day. Fidelity to
God requires that we adore God, and adore God with
others. Our salvation is not something we work at in
isolation from others.

Catholics take seriously Jesus' mandate to break
bread in his name. We gather weekly for community
worship and set aside a day when we slow down
from our other duties to create some time for rest and
reflection. Catholics typically worship on Sunday to
commemorate the day of the Lord's resurrection.

Keeping Sunday holy also retains the original
idea of Sabbath as a day of relaxation and renewal.

Catholics should refrain from unnecessary work and make time for the family and other wholesome activity on the Lord's day.

"Love Your Neighbor as Yourself"
(The Last Seven Commandments)

Honor your father and your mother. The covenant between Christians and God is reflected in the family. Just as God loves his children, so human parents should love and care for their children. And children should offer respect, obedience, courtesy, and gratitude to their parents. Likewise, brothers and sisters owe each other patience, friendship, and respect so that the family can be a harmonious community of love. This commandment also has social implications. All proper authority is deserving of our obedience and respect since all authority ultimately comes from God. And because authority comes from God, those in a position over others are obligated to exercise their authority with kindness and humility.

You shall not kill. God has given us the gift of life, and the fifth commandment stresses its sanctity. It condemns anything which assaults human life (for example, murder, suicide, drug trafficking). The values of the fifth commandment include taking care of ourselves, physically and mentally. Christians are also concerned about protecting the lives of others. Jesus showed that God's love extends in a special way to the weak and helpless. Thus, Christians should stand for peace, justice, and life by combatting war, poverty and prejudice, abortion and euthanasia, and the like.

You shall not commit adultery. Christian marriage is a powerful sign of covenant love. Infidelity is unbecoming to covenant love; in a marriage, adultery is a serious failure to be faithful to a love commitment.

The sixth commandment challenges us to respect the procreative powers with which God has blessed us. Sexual love is a share in God's own creative act. Acts which exploit others or which are indulged in selfishly distort God's intent. (See Chapter 16 for more information on a Christian approach to sexuality.)

You shall not steal. Theft of any kind destroys trust. To steal is to break down the smooth human relationships needed for harmonious and peaceful living. The seventh commandment also forbids cheating and abuse of the environment. It also reminds us to share the surplus goods we have been given with those who are in need. Not sharing with those who lack the very necessities of life is a serious failure to love.

You shall not bear false witness against your neighbor. To be honest is to witness to the truth. Revenge, gossip, scandal, lies, detraction (unnecessarily disclosing another's faults), and perjury all destroy the love which binds together the human community.

You shall not covet your neighbor's wife. You shall not covet anything that belongs to your neighbor. Covetousness is often motivated by lust, self-indulgence, envy, or greed. Uncontrolled desires in the areas of sex or material possessions can breed hatred, jealousy, and rivalry. These two commandments stress the importance of pure intentions and decent motives when relating to others. The external action which violates love usually flows from an internal desire which was left unchecked.

What are the Beatitudes?

The Beatitudes summarize the morality followers of Jesus should strive to live in response to both God and neighbor. They introduce and capsulize the essence of New Testament morality found in the Sermon on the Mount (Mt 5—7). The Beatitudes "are a sort of *self-portrait of Christ*"; they "are *invitations to discipleship and communion of life with Christ*" (Pope John Paul II, *The Splendor of Truth*, #16).

How blessed are the poor in spirit:, the kingdom of Heaven is theirs.

Blessed are the gentle: they shall have the earth as inheritance.

Blessed are those who mourn: they shall be comforted.

Blessed are those who hunger and thirst for uprightness: they shall have their fill.

Blessed are the merciful: they shall have mercy shown them.

Blessed are the pure in heart: they shall see God.

Blessed are the peacemakers: they shall be recognized as children of God.

Blessed are those who are persecuted in the cause of uprightness: the kingdom of Heaven is theirs (Mt 5:3-10).

How do we explain the Beatitudes?

How blessed are the poor in spirit: the kingdom of Heaven is theirs. In this beatitude Jesus is not praising poverty as such. Rather, he is saying that those who are deprived of material goods, power, prestige, and other signs of worldly success are left in a position of openness before God. They know they must trust God completely for everything. Jesus asks that we have that same poverty of spirit, that we place our trust and confidence in God alone.

Blessed are the gentle: they shall have the earth as inheritance. The gentle person is humble. He or she does not act out of jealousy or seek revenge when hurt and despised.

Blessed are those who mourn: they shall be comforted. The third beatitude gives us hope that in the midst of our difficulties we will eventually find consolation. We do not have to become bitter.

Blessed are those who hunger and thirst for uprightness: they shall have their fill. To "hunger and thirst for uprightness" means to seek divine justice, a good relationship with the perfectly upright, just, and righteous One. The eucharist can satisfy our appetite for holiness. It also impels us to treat others with justice, giving them their due and making sure that everyone has access to those things necessary for a truly human life.

Blessed are the merciful: they shall have mercy shown them. In the Our Father we ask God to forgive us as we forgive others. When we forgive those who have hurt us, even our enemies, we show all people that God is loving and merciful and that God cares for us all.

Blessed are the pure in heart: they shall see God. The pure in heart have a single-hearted commitment to God. Nothing should distract us from God. Money, job, family, friends, reputation are all good, but they should play a secondary role in our lives.

Blessed are the peacemakers: they shall be recognized as children of God. Lives lived in love and peace are the twin signs of being God's adopted children. Christians have the duty to unite those who are in strife, disharmony, and opposition by helping them realize our common brotherhood and sisterhood with Jesus Christ.

Blessed are those who are persecuted in the cause of uprightness: the kingdom of Heaven is theirs. There is no greater sign of our union with our Lord than being willing to suffer for him. Jesus' words and deeds brought him misunderstanding and abuse. To be Christian means to be willing to stand up for our convictions, even if this means rejection, abuse, or martyrdom.

10

THE CHURCH AND SOCIAL JUSTICE
Some Principles

The Lord's people, his church, are missionary. Our mission is threefold: to be the herald, the sign, and the servant of the gospel. We herald the good news when we proclaim the gospel of Jesus Christ. We are a sign of the gospel when we faithfully live the gospel. We serve the gospel when we witness to the message of God's saving love for the world. We do this best when we minister to people in need.

How are social justice and gospel love related?

Social justice deals with the application of the gospel to the structures, systems, and institutions of society. As stated in *Justice in the World*, "Love implies an absolute demand for justice, usually a recognition of the dignity and rights of one's neighbors." We cannot say we love if we do not respect and respond to the rights and basic needs of our neighbors. True love of God and neighbor are united.

In other words, to love means to give oneself to another. It is impossible to love without sharing with others what is due them in justice. Love can go beyond justice, however. Justice is simply the *minimal* human and Christian response to others. Love, if we are serious about becoming like Christ, requires going beyond justice.

What role has the church played in justice issues?

Throughout its history the church has attempted to show the link between the gospel and the plight of the poor. The Catholic church has often pioneered efforts on behalf of the poor and the powerless: home and foreign missions, hospitals and medical clinics, disaster relief agencies, orphanages, homes for unwed mothers, services for the elderly, agencies for young people, a massive educational apostolate.

There are those, however, who have criticized the church for not taking a more active role in promoting peace and justice. History shows that sometimes church leaders did neglect the social dimension of the gospel while preaching quiet acceptance of their misery to the poor and oppressed.

In our day the church has taken a leading role in the promotion of justice:

Action on behalf of justice and participation in the transformation of the world fully appear to us as a constitutive dimension of the preaching of the Gospel, or in other words, of the Church's mission of the redemption of the human race and its liberation from every oppressive situation (Introduction to *Justice in the World*).

This important document makes it clear that working for justice in the world ranks with the celebration of the sacraments and the preaching of the gospel as an essential ministry in the church.

What are the basics of the church's social teaching?

In their pastoral message *A Century of Social Teaching: A Common Heritage, A Continuing Challenge*, the American bishops outline six basic themes that undergird Catholic social teaching:

1. The church upholds the life and dignity of the individual.

2. The church recognizes that there are certain basic human rights with their corresponding duties.

3. The church recognizes that human beings are by nature social and that God calls us to family, community, and service.

4. The church recognizes the truth of human solidarity and that all humans belong to one family, God's family.

5. The church endorses the dignity of work and the rights of workers.

6. The church teaches a preferential option for the poor and vulnerable.

What is meant by "the dignity of the individual"?

Catholic social teaching roots itself in the human person. Each of us images and reflects God. Jesus loves and redeems all humans. All have basic dignity and are "capable of knowing and loving their Creator" (*The Church in the Modern World*, #12) who made us for interpersonal communication. Our worth comes from *who we are* as God's children, not *what we do*. Nor is our worth dependent on race, gender, age, or economic status. Catholic social teaching would have us judge every policy, law, and institution according to how they enhance human life and dignity.

What are our rights and duties?

Justice demands that a society be organized in a way that guarantees everyone the ability to participate in its political, cultural, and economic life. Basic human rights are prerequisites to living a life of dignity in community. Among the major human rights which have been discussed and defended in a number of church documents are the following:

Economic rights
- right to life: food, shelter, clothing, medical care
- right to work
- right to a just wage
- right to property

Political and social rights
- right to participate in government
- right to judicial protection
- right to assembly

Religious and cultural rights
- right to worship
- right to a basic education
- right to freedom of speech

Every right has a corresponding duty for each person to respect, foster, and fulfill. For example, the right to participate in government carries the duty to cast an informed vote in elections.

In what way are humans social beings?

God created us as members of the human family. We are by nature *social*. From the beginning God created us for companionship. The progress of the human person and the advance of society are interdependent. We belong to three communities that are like concentric circles: the individual lives in the circle of the family, which is part of a larger circle, the nation, which is part of the largest circle, the world. These are the communities most often discussed in the church's social teaching.

What is the call to human solidarity?

Our solidarity with each other and our world encompasses issues like world peace, global development, environmental issues, and international human rights. Violent conflict and the denial of human rights to people anywhere affects and diminishes us all. We simply must hear the call of others, especially the weak in our midst. Jesus unites the love of God and love of neighbor. He prayed for human solidarity:

"May they all be one,
just as, Father, you are in me and I am in you" (Jn 17:21).

What is the relationship between the dignity of work and the rights of workers?

Work helps us make a living, expresses our human dignity, and helps us participate in God's ongoing creation. Work must be for people, not people for work. We have the basic right to decent and productive work, fair wages, private property, and economic initiative. The church has consistently upheld workers' right to form unions and associations in their pursuit of their rights and dignity, and the belief that the economy exists to help people, not vice versa.

What is the "preferential option for the poor"?

Catholic social teaching asks society this question: How are its most vulnerable members faring? Jesus taught in the Last Judgment scene (Mt 25) that we must put the needs of the poor and vulnerable first. Pope John Paul II has expressed well the link between justice and the love of the poor:

Justice will never be fully attained unless people see in the poor person, who is asking for help in order to survive, not an annoyance or a burden, but an opportunity for showing kindness and a chance for greater enrichment. ... It is not enough to draw on the surplus good which in fact our world abundantly produces; it requires above all a change of lifestyles, of models of production and consumption, and of the established structures of power which today govern societies (*The One Hundredth Year*, #58).

11

SOCIAL JUSTICE
Building on the Foundations

Catholic moral teaching is interested in social justice because social justice applies the gospel command to respect and love others to the concrete reality of everyday life. The Christian gospel is not meant to be a vague, idealistic statement with no connection to how people live their lives. Rather, the good news of Jesus demands application to the social settings in which we find ourselves: the family, the nation, and the world.

What does the church teach about the family?

The bedrock unit of any society is the family. Its special value lies in its willingness to affirm and to love individuals not for what they can accomplish or the possessions they own but simply for who they are. Married couples in a Christian, sacramental union model Christ's own love for the church. His love is enduring and self-giving. Marriage is both love-sharing between the couple and life-giving. The twin values of life and love provide a strong foundation for the larger society.

What principles undergird church teaching on national concerns?

All nations must be concerned about social issues, problems, and rights in order to foster the common good. The topics discussed below—respect for the unborn, women in society, respect for racial and ethnic groups, employment, and poverty—are frequently addressed in papal documents and in the letters of national conferences of bishops.

What is the church's stance regarding the unborn?

Jesus taught in the strongest of terms the need to care for the weak and the helpless. For the sake of the common good, the fundamental right to life itself must be first recognized and then protected by law. Efforts to correct legal decisions which permit abortion on demand, for example, are one means to remedy the assault on human life.

Furthermore, society needs to offer help and assistance to those women who feel that the only way out of their current problem is through abortion. The church, especially because of its pro-life stance, should be in the forefront in supporting women with problems during or after pregnancy and thus bear strong witness to its belief in human dignity.

Respect and reverence for human life arise from the basic dignity of the human person made in God's image and likeness. Life is a most precious gift from God. Abortion is gravely wrong, as is any direct attack on human life like infanticide, euthanasia, and certain kinds of fetal experiments.

What is the church's stance regarding women in modern society?

Jesus recognized the equality and dignity of women. The church praises those efforts which win recognition that women have the same dignity and fundamental rights as men.

> With respect to the fundamental rights of the person, every type of discrimination, whether social or cultural, whether based on sex, race, color or social condition, language, or religion, is to be overcome and eradicated as contrary to God's intent (*The Church in the Modern World*, #29).

What is the church's stance regarding racial and ethnic groups?

All racial and ethnic groups are of incomparable worth because of their dignity as human beings. Yet individuals and the structures of society often discriminate to the disadvantage of innocent people. It is true that laws cannot change attitudes, but they can foster justice by protecting minority groups, by deterring those who might otherwise violate the rights of others, and by educating people to know right from wrong.

What is the church's stance on employment?

The church has spoken loudly and clearly on the rights of workers:

> Every [person] has the right to work, to a chance to develop his qualities and his personality in the exercise of his profession, to equitable remuneration which will enable him and his family "to lead a worthy life on the material, social, cultural, and spiritual level" and to assistance in case of need arising from sickness or age (*A Call to Action*, #14).

What does the church teach about poverty?

The American bishops define poverty as "the lack of sufficient material resources required for a decent life" (*Economic Justice for All*, #173). Children, female-headed households, and members of racial minorities are victimized by poverty to a greater degree than other groups.

The American bishops' pastoral letter on the economy makes a number of concrete recommendations on how the plight of the poor can be helped. These include raising the minimum wage, adjustment in the tax system to better meet the needs of the poor, a major commitment to education and the eradication of illiteracy, better support of the family so that mothers of young children are not forced to seek employment outside the home, and a thorough reform of the welfare system.

What is the special threat of consumerism?

Consumerism leads to materialism which, in turn, leaves people empty. The media contributes to the message that the more one has the more one needs. Consumerism, which hurts the poor, makes people self-centered and fails to fulfill their true human destiny or needs. Pope John Paul II has written:

> It is not wrong to want to live better; what is wrong is a style of life which is presumed to be better when it is directed toward "having" rather than "being" and which wants to have more, not in order to be more, but in order to spend life in enjoyment as an end in itself (*The One Hundredth Year*, #36).

What other national problems has the church addressed?

Crime and criminals. People have the right and need to live in peace and to be protected from criminals. Societies should work not only at stricter law enforcement but should also strive to root out the sources of much crime—poverty, injustice, and materialism.

Prisoners, too, have rights: They have the right to protection from assault; the right to proper food, health care, and recreation; and the right to pursue other human goals such as education.

Migrant workers. Justice in the World especially laments the condition of migrant workers who are frequently the victims of discriminatory attitudes and are often obliged to live insecure lives. Emigrating to find work is sometimes a necessary evil, but "migration in search of work must in no way become an opportunity for financial or social exploitation" (*On Human Work*, #23).

Communications. The people who control media have a "grave responsibility with respect to the truth of the information they spread, the needs and the reactions they generate, and the values they put forward" (*A Call to Action*, #20). In this regard the American bishops suggest that the government can help create more wholesome societies by taking "constitutional steps to stem the flood of pornography, violence, and immorality in the entertainment media" (*To Live in Christ Jesus*, p. 30).

Environment. When God entrusted the human race with the development of the created world, God made us stewards of his magnificent creation (Gn 1:28-30). This is a tremendous responsibility. Yet today we have become more aware that we have exploited nature, and we risk destroying it. Pollution, refuse, scarcity of vital natural resources, and new illnesses result from an unchecked technology fueled by human selfishness and greed. Responsibility demands careful planning, conservation, and an unselfish respect for the goods of this world.

What does the church teach on world problems?

Our concern for the rights of others does not stop with the family or with our own nation. To follow Jesus means to love all people. The Christian in today's world must also show concern for the international community. Christian love and justice prompt us to extend care beyond our national borders.

The world is in dire need of help. Some of the problems which loom on the horizon include hunger, environmental pollution, population growth, disparity of wealth and resources, and the persistent danger of war.

What is the church's response to these global issues?

Pope John Paul II calls on individuals, leaders, societies, and nations to convert and turn away from greed and consumerism and to make a wholehearted commitment to work to the development of every human being. True development begins with love of God and love of neighbor, and love manifests itself in respect for all God's creatures which make up our natural world. Of major concern to the church in our day has been the right of nations to develop and become liberated from oppressive practices and situations which keep the poor in their dependent and often hopeless conditions.

A constant theme in papal teaching concerning developing nations has been the right of those nations and peoples to control and direct their own process of development. The right to develop includes economic growth as well as political, social, and economic participation in the process of development.

The church likewise teaches that to be disciples of Jesus Christ means to be passionately devoted to peace. Peace is not merely the absence of war. It is an enterprise of justice and must be built up ceaselessly.

12

SACRAMENTS
A Life of Grace

We need symbols because we are body-people. We need concrete signs to express mysteries like love. We need to say and to hear loving words, to give and receive gifts, to kiss and be kissed, to shake hands, to write and receive notes of appreciation. This is true in our relationships with other people; it is also true in our relationship with God.

Sacraments and a sacramental life are absolutely central to Catholic identity and belief. To reflect on their meaning and to appreciate what they represent—God's presence to us in our ordinary life—is to grow in an understanding of what Catholics hold to be very precious. In a real sense, the sacraments are an embodiment of the good news of God's love.

What is a sacrament?

A *sacrament* is an "efficacious symbol," that is, a special kind of symbol that causes what it points to, what it represents. As we saw in Chapter 7, this definition fits both Jesus and his church. The seven sacraments are special actions of Christ working in the church. They are effective, symbolic actions which not only point to God's life but actually convey it to the members of the church. They bring about what they point to.

What are these symbols of God's love for us?

The Catholic church recognizes seven sacraments. We believe that the Lord has left the Christian community with these seven signs of love which touch us during the key moments of our lives. When we begin life, *baptism* unites us with the risen Lord and all our fellow Christians. As we mature and begin to more fully accept and live the Christian life, *confirmation* showers us with the strength of the Holy Spirit to live faithfully for the Lord. The *eucharist*, the sacred meal which commemorates and re-enacts the Lord's sacrifice on the cross for our salvation, symbolizes and brings about our union with God.

When we are guilty of sin and in need of reconciliation and forgiveness, we experience the Lord's forgiving love in the sacrament of *reconciliation*. And in times of serious illness, the *anointing of the sick* gives us God's mercy, forgiveness, courage, and hope.

Jesus is with us as we live out our life's vocation. Those who are called to serve God's people as deacons, priests, or bishops are supported through the sacrament of *holy orders*. And the sacrament of *matrimony* is an ongoing sign of God's love as it appears in the union of a couple who are committed to loving each other until death. Their union and their fidelity are signs of the Lord's union with us and his faithfulness to his church.

What does a sacrament do?

A sacrament makes visible the mystery of God's love for us. The seven sacraments renew the mystery of God's love. As the council fathers taught:

> [Their purpose] is to sanctify, to build up the body of Christ, and finally, to give worship to God. Because they are signs, they also instruct. They not only presuppose faith, but by words and objects they also nourish, strengthen, and express it (*Constitution on the Sacred Liturgy*, No. 59).

What is the traditional definition of *sacrament*?

The *Catechism of the Catholic Church* (#1131) reaffirms a classic definition of the term *sacrament*: an efficacious sign of grace, instituted by Christ and entrusted to the church, by which divine life is dispensed to us.

Efficacious sign. St. Augustine defined a sacrament as a "visible sign of invisible grace." Through words and actions we can sense, experience, and come to believe spiritual realities that exist beyond our senses. We know that something important is happening behind these outward signs, which bring about what they point to. We are celebrating Christ's presence; God's friendship with God's people is entering our lives.

Instituted by Christ and entrusted to the church. Jesus came to preach the good news and establish his Father's kingdom. With the guidance and power of the Holy Spirit, the church has developed the seven sacraments as special, unique signs whose purpose is to build up the kingdom of God. God's action, not human action, accounts for the Christian sacraments.

To confer grace, God's life to us. The purpose of the sacraments is to convey grace. *Grace* is a traditional Catholic term which refers to our participating in God's life. Grace is God's free gift of friendship, God's help that enables us to live as God's adopted daughters and sons.

Sacraments are not magical rituals. They presuppose openness, faith, and cooperation on our part. We must respond to them and live the gift of God's life which God offers to us.

The sacraments are perceptible signs (words and actions) accessible to our human nature. By action of Christ and the power of the Holy Spirit

they make present efficaciously the grace that
they signify (*CCC*, #1084).

What is liturgy?

Public worship of God is known as *liturgy*, a
word which originally meant "the people's work."
Liturgy is the official public worship of the church.
It includes the sacraments, recitation of the Liturgy
of the Hours, and the liturgical year. Christian liturgy uses words, actions, and symbols to celebrate the
presence of God in our midst. It reminds us of who
we are and what we are in relation to our loving
God. Through it we bless and worship God as the
source of all the blessings of creation and salvation.

It is the mystery of Christ that the Church
proclaims and celebrates in her liturgy so that
the faithful may live from it and bear witness to
it in the world (*CCC*, #1068).

Liturgy is organized into *ritual*. All rituals bring
a recognizable order to certain words, actions, and
symbols in order to create a meaningful celebration
for a particular group. The seven sacraments are
important rituals of the church.

13

THE SACRAMENTS
OF INITIATION

The sacraments of initiation help "gather in" God's people, incorporating them into the Body of Christ, the Christian community that is the church. Like all sacraments, they powerfully commission God's chosen ones to be Christ for the world. These sacraments confer the life of Jesus, they bestow the gift of the Spirit on the People of God so that they can continue the Lord's mission in word and deed to a world that is hungering for meaning and love.

What are the sacraments of initiation?

The sacraments of baptism, confirmation, and eucharist are known as the sacraments of initiation. Most American Catholics were baptized as infants, received first communion in second grade, and were confirmed either in junior or senior high school. In early Christian times most converts were adults who celebrated all three sacraments of initiation at one time after participating in a lengthy formation period—often three years—called the *catechumenate*. With their sponsors these *catechumens* learned about the Christian faith and became disciplined to the Christian way of life through prayer, fasting, and self-denial. This ancient way of initiating adults into the Christian community has been revived in our own day through the *Rite of Christian Initiation of Adults (RCIA)*.

What is the RCIA?

The *RCIA* is a process which has four periods and three rites, outlined and briefly described below.

Period 1: Precatechumenate. The journey to Christian initiation begins with a period of inquiry. The inquirers share life experiences with Catholics, reflect on the scriptural word of God, seek knowledge about the Catholic religion and its relationship to Christianity, and learn about Jesus Christ.

Stage 1: Rite of Acceptance. Through a rite of welcome, the seekers ask for acceptance into the Catholic faith community, and they are joyfully accepted into the church as candidates for Christian initiation. They become known as *catechumens.*

Period 2: Catechumenate. After the initial celebration of welcoming, the catechumens study the Christian faith more deeply (sometimes under the guidance of a sponsor, a caring role model for how a Christian lives). Catechumens grow familiar with the Christian way of life, study the scriptures, participate fully in the liturgy of the word, and begin to take an active role in the life of the community.

Stage 2: Rite of Election. On the first Sunday of Lent the "elect" gather at their parish and are called forward to take the final steps toward Christian initiation. Later in the day they travel to the cathedral where all the catechumens in the diocese are enrolled as the elect who will be baptized at the Easter vigil and fully received into the community.

Period 3: Purification and Enlightenment. During this period the elect are challenged to prepare themselves for baptism and full reception into the community by prayer and fasting during Lent.

During the Sundays of Lent there are special rituals and prayers for the elect. Reflection on the Sunday readings, especially from John's gospel, helps the baptismal candidates choose Jesus and his kingdom over the way of Satan and darkness. The elect also learn the Christian creed and the Lord's

Prayer, the basic summary of Christian beliefs and the prayer of all those who follow Christ.

Stage 3: Rite of Initiation. The rite of initiation typically takes place during the Easter vigil liturgy. The elect are baptized, confirmed, and receive eucharist for the first time as full members of Christ's body. Baptism includes a litany, the blessing of water, the baptism itself, clothing in a white garment, and the presentation of a candle lit from the paschal candle. Confirmation includes words of prayer, the imposition of hands, and the anointing with the blessed oils.

Period 4: Mystagogia. During the weeks following Easter Sunday, the new Christians meet to reflect on the meaning of the recent events in their lives as Christians. They are supported by the community through a deeper study into the mysteries of the faith, those signs of God's love present in the church's life and in the lives of Christians.

Pentecost Sunday concludes the catechumenate and begins the lifelong pilgrimage of a fully initiated Christian. They now have the full responsibility of a follower of Jesus.

What is baptism?

The church baptizes because Christ himself commanded it:

"Go, therefore, make disciples of all nations; baptize them in the name of the Father and of the Son and of the Holy Spirit" (Mt 28:19).

Baptism is a sign of God's love for us. Through baptism, we symbolically enter into the mystery of Christ's death and resurrection. The church calls us to die to sin and accept a new life of redemption in Jesus. Baptism initiates us into the Body of Christ. It forgives sin and gives us the support of the Christian community to live Christlike lives. It configures us to Christ and seals us with an indelible spiritual character; thus, baptism cannot be repeated.

How is baptism of a child administered?

When parents present their children for baptism, they profess that they are willing to raise their children with gospel values. The godparents (one of whom must be an active, fully initiated Catholic) and fellow parishioners promise to support the parents in their commitment. It is appropriately celebrated at a Sunday liturgy; it should always be celebrated in an assembly of Christian believers.

The ceremony begins with a greeting from the ordained minister. The minister then welcomes the child by making the sign of the cross on the child's forehead, inviting parents and godparents to do the same. After the liturgy of the word, he blesses the baptismal water and leads the parents, godparents, and the Christians assembled to profess their faith and renew their baptismal vows on their own behalf and on behalf of the child.

The minister pours water on the head of the child (or immerses the child in water) and pronounces the words:

I baptize you in the name of the Father,
and of the Son,
and of the Holy Spirit.

Following the baptism the child's forehead is anointed with oil, a white garment is placed on the child, and a candle lit from the paschal candle is held by one of the godparents. All assembled recite the Our Father after which the celebrant concludes the ceremony by blessing the mother, then the father, and finally the entire congregation.

What do the symbols of baptism signify?

Water. "To baptize" means to plunge or immerse (in water). Water symbolizes life, cleansing, and death. Baptismal water means the death of an old life to sin and the rebirth into a new life with Jesus Christ. Original sin is washed away, and we inherit eternal life as adopted children of God.

Oil. Oil heals and protects. The anointing with oil reminds us that the Lord extends salvation to us and sends the Spirit to protect and strengthen us. The root meaning of *Christ* is "anointed one." The oil of baptism symbolizes that we have been "Christened." We become the anointed of the Anointed One.

White garment. In the early church Christians put on new white robes as they emerged from the baptismal pool. Today, by putting on this symbol of purity, festivity, and new identity, the baptized person shows a willingness to live a new life in union with the Lord.

Light. A beautiful part of the baptismal liturgy is the giving of a candle to the newly baptized. The celebrant lights this candle from the paschal (Easter) candle, a symbol of Christ. The baptismal candle challenges us to be the light of Christ, to live lovingly so others can see Christ working in the world.

In the name of. The church baptizes us in the name of the Blessed Trinity, thus signifying adoption into the divine family. In the reception rite of the baptismal liturgy, the celebrant asks for the baptismal name of the candidate. Christians usually take the name of a patron saint. Looking to the saints for inspiration and help reveals our faith in the communion of saints.

What happens to the unbaptized?

The church teaches that some form of baptism in Jesus Christ is necessary for salvation. Traditionally the church has taught there are three forms of baptism: baptism by water (through the rite), baptism by blood (the death of martyrs), and baptism by desire. Baptism by desire refers to those who were not granted the gift of faith but whose lives show that they would have accepted Jesus if they had the chance.

> Those who die for the faith, those who are catechumens, and all those who, without knowing of the Church but acting under the inspiration of grace, seek God sincerely and strive to fulfill his will, are saved even if they have not been baptized (CCC, #1281).

What is confirmation?

Confirmation is a sacrament of initiation. Confirmation brings to completion the making of a Christian. It is the seal of baptism, a celebration of the gift of the Holy Spirit, and a confirming of the baptismal gifts given by the Spirit. Adults are confirmed at the Easter vigil liturgy immediately after their baptism; children who were baptized as infants are usually confirmed some years afterward.

How is the rite of confirmation celebrated?

Confirmation usually takes place during a eucharistic liturgy to stress the relationship among the sacraments of initiation. After the liturgy of the word, the presentation of the candidates, and a short homily or instruction, the bishop—the ordinary minister of this sacrament—and the concelebrating priests extend their hands over the candidates as the bishop invokes the outpouring of the Holy Spirit.

Each candidate then comes before the bishop who moistens his thumb with the oil of chrism, makes the sign of the cross on the candidate's forehead, and says:

N., be sealed with the Gift of the Holy Spirit.
A greeting of peace and general intercessions conclude the rite before continuing the Mass.

The anointing with chrism—the mixture of olive oil and perfume that the bishop blesses on Holy Thursday—symbolizes that the goodness of the newly confirmed must permeate the world. Oil, a symbol of strength, is also a sign of holiness, of one specially chosen by God. The anointing in the sign of the cross on the forehead stresses how a Christian should resemble Jesus Christ and boldly witness to him.

What are the major effects of confirmation?

1. Confirmation confers and seals the fullness of the Holy Spirit. To be "sealed" means to become stamped as belonging to someone. At confirmation we become official ambassadors of Jesus, empowered by the Holy Spirit, and conformed more perfectly to Christ. Confirmation imprints a permanent spiritual mark; thus, we can receive it only once.

2. Confirmation strengthens us to live as Christians. "To confirm" means "to ratify" and "to strengthen." Confirmation perfects the graces of baptism and grounds us more deeply in our relationship as God's children.

Today, confirmation is often celebrated by adolescents on their way to adulthood. Thus, theologians frequently call confirmation "the sacrament of maturity." The Lord calls young adults and adults alike to courageously witness to the paschal mystery.

3. Confirmation deepens the power of the gifts received in baptism. The Holy Spirit endows us with gifts that strengthen us and enable us to do Christ's work (see Chapter 5 for more on the gifts).

What is the eucharist?

The eucharist is the greatest sacrament of the church. It is the prime symbol of love and completes the process of Christian initiation. We will learn about it in the next chapter.

14

SACRAMENTS
The Eucharist

The eucharist is the central act of worship in the liturgical life of the Catholic church. The celebration of the holy sacrifice of the Mass is the best expression of the church's worship of God. Eucharist means "thanksgiving." It is the sublime means Christians have of thanking God the Father for the gift of his Son, Jesus Christ.

What does the eucharist represent?

The eucharist is an efficacious symbol, instituted by Jesus Christ, which symbolizes what it brings about and brings about what it symbolizes. Among other things, the eucharist represents and brings about the following: spiritual life and nourishment; the sacrifice of love which sanctifies; Christian community and unity; the presence of Jesus Christ in the life of the individual and the Christian community; the paschal mystery which brings eternal life.

How is the eucharist a sacred meal?

The eucharist is a commemorative meal which recalls the Last Supper Jesus celebrated with his apostles. A meal has an intimate quality about it. Those who share the joy of companionship gather and partake of the same food. The word companionship means "breaking bread together." A shared meal is a universal symbol of friendship.

Jesus was aware of the deep meaning associated with meals when he instituted the eucharist at a traditional Jewish Passover. The Passover meal reminded the Jewish people of God's goodness and fidelity to the divine promise of rescuing them from Egypt. It is no accident that our Lord presents himself in the form of food and drink. Food and drink are necessary for human survival; they remind us that without their ultimate source, God, we would surely die. So, too, without the sharing of our brother and savior Jesus Christ, we would spiritually die.

The eucharist foreshadows our spiritual inheritance, the heavenly banquet where we will be united totally with God and with our brothers and sisters.

What does the eucharistic bread symbolize?

Bread is a symbol of life. It is the ordinary food for vast numbers of human beings. Consecrated bread at the eucharist, transformed mysteriously into the body of the Lord Jesus, is life itself.

The use of unleavened bread at Mass carries rich meaning. In the context of the Passover meal that Jesus was celebrating with his disciples, unleavened bread was a reminder of the haste with which the Jews had escaped from Egypt in the time of Moses. They didn't even have time to let the bread rise. We use unleavened bread to remind us that we are a pilgrim people. We have not yet arrived at our heavenly kingdom. We are utterly dependent on God's help.

What does the eucharistic wine symbolize?

In many cultures, wine is the ordinary drink at meals. It has a joyous, communal quality about it. Consecrated wine is the Lord's blood. Blood in the scriptures is often a sign of life uniting God with his people. Jesus offered his blood as a sign of the new covenant between God and his people.

How is the eucharist a sacrifice?

Another key symbol of the Passover meal was the paschal lamb, which the Jews offered as a sacrifice to God. Jesus became the new paschal lamb, the perfect victim who offered his life for all people. The Passover meal signified the old covenant; Jesus' sacrificial death and resurrection inaugurate the new covenant.

Sacrifice comes from a Latin word which means "to make holy" or "to do something holy." Holiness refers to sharing God's life, being, and love. Only God can make us holy. The purpose of sacrificing to God is to adore God, to acknowledge God as the source of our life and the creator of all. We also sacrifice to atone for our sins, to give thanks for God's goodness, and to petition God for favors.

The altar wonderfully represents the meal and sacrificial symbolism of the eucharist. It is the altar of sacrifice and the table of the Lord. Additionally, it symbolizes Christ himself, present in the assembly both as the victim offered for our reconciliation and as our heavenly food.

Catholics believe that Jesus himself instituted the eucharistic sacrifice at the Last Supper. The eucharist represents Christ's sacrifice on the cross, the supreme sign of his love for us. Jesus, God's Son, is also the perfect human being, our representative before God. Through him, all humans receive and respond to God's offer of love. Jesus put himself in his Father's hands. Surrendering himself obediently, he gave up his life for all people.

What is the meaning of the eucharistic sacrifice?

When we offer the sacrifice of the Mass, we continue to be made holy by accepting and living the example of our brother and savior Jesus Christ. His freely accepted death shows us that love is the way to holiness. When we remember, celebrate, and attempt to live his sacrifice—his way of love—we ourselves are changed by God into more loving people.

In what sense is the eucharist the "blessed sacrament"?

The eucharist is the heart of Catholic life. It is the source, center, and summit of the whole life of the church. It is the prime sacrament, the one from which all others come and the one to which the others point. We call this sacrament "blessed," a biblical word which means a communication of God's life to us. "Blessed sacrament" is an apt name for the sacrament which gives us Christ himself.

Why do we call the eucharist "holy communion"?

Communion means "union with." Communion with Jesus unites us with God and all other Christians. It gives us power to live loving lives for the Lord. The church encourages us to receive the food of salvation at eucharistic celebrations. We should do so worthily and with knowledge of what the eucharist is. Worthy reception means being free from mortal sin and fasting from food and drink for at least an hour before reception (except for water and medicine).

When we receive Christ in the eucharist, we become one with the Lord Jesus. His life enters us and transforms us. Communion with Christ preserves, increases, and renews baptismal graces. It strengthens us spiritually, forgives venial sin, and helps preserve us from future mortal sin. Receiving Christ in holy communion also enables us to recognize Christ in the poorest of his brothers and sisters.

Holy communion also unites us more closely to our Christian brothers and sisters. We receive the body of Christ to become the Body of Christ. As the sign and cause of unity, the eucharist impels us to unity with all Christians. Receiving the Lord also enables us to share in the spiritual riches of all those heroic Christians who have gone before us.

What is meant by the "real presence"?

Catholics hold that Jesus is truly present in the community assembled for worship. We also believe that he is present in the priest who presides over the eucharist in his name, and in the proclamation of the word. But in addition, we believe that Jesus is present in a special way in the sacred species of bread and wine.

Exactly how Jesus is present in the consecrated bread and wine is a mystery. The church has used the word *transubstantiation* to express that at the consecration of the Mass the reality (the substance) of the bread and wine change into the reality of Jesus—his risen, glorified body and blood. To receive Jesus in the "species" of the bread or the "species" of the wine is to receive the whole Christ since he is totally present in both species.

Catholics also believe that our Lord's presence endures in the sacred species of the blessed sacrament. In Catholic churches the blessed sacrament is reserved in the tabernacle, a safe-like, secure receptacle usually located in a chapel or on a side altar. A traditional devotion to our Lord is visiting him in the blessed sacrament.

How is the eucharist a celebration?

We celebrate many things at Mass, but especially we celebrate the paschal mystery, that is, the passion, death, resurrection, and glorification of Jesus Christ. At Mass the assembled community rejoices in our Lord's risen presence and the power of his love which binds all people together. The eucharist is a celebration of praise, worship, and thanksgiving to our God.

What does the word "Mass" mean?

The term Mass is derived from the Latin words recited at the dismissal *"Ite missa est"* which mean "Go, you are sent." This reminds us of our duty to love and serve the Lord in all the people we meet. When we "break bread" in the name of Jesus, we are celebrating our brotherhood and sisterhood and receiving the source of our life, the Lord Jesus. In this sacred meal, he reminds us to take him out into the world, a world that desperately needs his love.

How is the eucharist a ritual?

The liturgy of the Mass is a ritual. It is a renewal of the new covenant in Jesus Christ. It enables us to enter into the events we celebrate. The ritual of the eucharist is a patterned remembering of the events Jesus enacted for our salvation. The liturgy of the eucharist does three things: 1) It celebrates, recalls, and commemorates the *past* of our salvation—the life, death, and resurrection of Jesus; 2) it celebrates the paschal mystery which is happening *right now* in our midst; and 3) it looks to the *future* of the church and the ultimate life with the Lord in heaven.

What are the parts of the Mass?

The Mass consists of the introductory rites, the liturgy of the word, the liturgy of the eucharist, and the concluding rites. In the liturgy of the word we hear the word of God and derive nourishment from it. We are challenged to make it part of our lives and to respond to it. In the liturgy of the eucharist we celebrate the death and resurrection of Jesus. We fully participate in the eucharist when we receive the Lord under the forms of bread and wine.

Introductory Rites

Entrance: The Mass begins with the singing or recitation of a song.

Greeting: The priest and people make the sign of the cross. The priest greets the people, and they respond.

Penitential Rite: The priest and people acknowledge their sinfulness and ask God's forgiveness.

Hymn of Praise (not always part of the Mass): The "Glory to God" is sung or recited.

Opening Prayer: The priest offers a prayer of petition on behalf of the worshipping community.

Liturgy of the Word

Readings: The first reading is usually from the Old Testament; the second from the latter part of the New Testament; the third from one of the gospels. Psalm verses are recited between the readings and alleluias are sung before the gospel.

Homily: The celebrant or deacon relates the readings to everyday life.

Profession of Faith (not always part of the Mass): Together the people acknowledge their common beliefs.

General Intercessions: The community's petitions for the needs of the church, the world, public authorities, individuals, and the local community are presented.

Liturgy of the Eucharist

Preparation of the Altar and Gifts: The gifts of bread and wine are brought forward in procession, the altar is prepared, and a prayer is said over the gifts.

Eucharistic Prayer (Canon): There are several eucharistic prayers that are used on different occasions. The eucharistic prayer includes the words Jesus said at the Last Supper, the memorial acclamation, and concludes with the doxology, praise to the Trinity sung or recited by the celebrant.

Communion Rite: This part of the Mass includes the Lord's Prayer, the prayer for deliverance, the prayer for peace (after which the sign of peace is exchanged), and the breaking of the bread while the Lamb of God is sung or recited. After the reception of communion, the priest offers a prayer of petition on behalf of the community.

Concluding Rite

Announcements

Dismissal

What is the "Sunday obligation"?

In the early church celebrating the eucharist was a privilege. But as the centuries progressed, the church had to pass a law to remind Catholics of their obligation to worship the Lord weekly in the eucharist. Weekly attendance at Sunday or Saturday evening Mass is now a fundamental aspect of Catholic life. Going to Mass, even when it is difficult to do so or when we simply do not feel like going, is to show love to God and to our fellow pilgrims. We share ourselves and publicly proclaim that we want to worship and thank God for everything God has given to us, especially our salvation through his Son Jesus.

Recall the meaning of liturgy as "the people's work." Jesus himself tells us that to be his followers, we must walk the extra mile, stand out, be different. The Christian life is also a communal life. We need the help, encouragement, and love of others. Above all, we need the Lord. We need the word of God to nourish and challenge us. We need the eucharistic Lord himself to transform us and make us like himself.

15

THE SACRAMENTS OF HEALING
Reconciliation and Anointing of the Sick

To live means to be well. With mental and spiritual health in mind, the Christian might even add, "To live means to be good." Sometimes we are not good, though. We sin. Our spiritual health suffers. We become alienated from God, others, and ourselves. At other times we are not physically well. Our bodies are sick with disease, the aches and pains of old age, the inevitable decline toward death.

Our Lord Jesus left with us two powerful signs of his love. He knows both our spiritual and physical sicknesses, and he has come to restore us to health. The Lord continues his work of healing today in the sacraments of reconciliation and the anointing of the sick.

What is the scriptural basis for the sacrament of reconciliation?

Jesus came to forgive sin and to heal people of the wounded relationships which sin causes. He empowered his church to continue his ministry of healing and reconciliation when he commanded his disciples to forgive sin in his name:

"Receive the Holy Spirit.
If you forgive anyone's sins,
they are forgiven;
if you retain anyone's sins,
they are retained" (Jn 20:23).

What are the traditional names for this sacrament?

The church has called this sacrament the sacrament of penance, confession, forgiveness, or reconciliation. We call it the sacrament of penance (a word meaning conversion) because it consecrates the individual sinner's and the church's steps of conversion, penance, and satisfaction. We call it confession because the telling of our sins to a priest is an essential part of the sacrament. The sacrament is also a wonderful confession—recognition and praise—of God's mercy to us. Similarly, we call it the sacrament of forgiveness since God grants pardon and peace to sinners through the words of absolution. Finally, reconciliation means "coming back together." This term for the sacrament emphasizes our need to repair the harmed relationships with God and others that our sins have caused.

What are the key elements of the sacrament of reconciliation?

The sacrament of reconciliation includes three acts of the penitent—contrition, confession, and satisfaction (penance)—and the words of absolution announced by the priest. An important preliminary step is a good examination of conscience in which the Holy Spirit helps us uncover areas of sinfulness in our lives. A reflection on the Sermon on the Mount, the Ten Commandments, and Christ's call to love God, neighbor, and self can help show us how we need Christ's healing touch.

What is contrition?

Contrition is "heartfelt sorrow and aversion for the sin committed along with the intention of sinning no more" (*Decree on Penance*, #6). Contrition is the heart of conversion which brings us back to God who is our loving, forgiving Father. Contrition enables us to approach the sacrament with the joy and expectation of God's own child.

Why "confess" our sins?

Confession is an external sign of interior sorrow. Through it, we meet the Christian community in the person of the priest and face our own sinful condition in the eyes of God. Confession also forces sin out into the open, thus emphasizing its social nature. We should always confess keeping in mind God's loving mercy.

The church requires us to confess the serious sins of which we are aware by number and kind at least once a year. The sacrament of reconciliation is the sole, ordinary means for Catholics conscious of mortal sin to be reconciled with God and the church. In this sacrament, Christ tells each person individually: "I forgive you. Go in peace."

The church does not strictly require the confession of venial sins. But we should use this sacrament for venial sins because the sacrament of penance is the church's most important form of reconciliation. Sacramental confession heightens our sense of sin, conforms us to Christ, and puts us in touch with the Holy Spirit who calls us to holiness. And frequent recourse to this sacrament helps us uproot sin from our lives.

What is the value of penance?

If we have true conversion, we want to make up for our sins, amend our lives, and repair any injuries we have caused. The priest assigns a penance to help us correct the harm done or to serve as a spiritual remedy for our sins. We should accept and joyfully perform these acts of satisfaction, such as prayers and good works.

What is absolution?

The priest serves as the Lord's representative and announces the words of absolution on behalf of the church. When the priest holds his hands over the penitent's head and recites the words, "I absolve you from your sins in the name of the Father, and of the Son, and of the Holy Spirit," Christ himself is giving us the sign we as humans need to know that we are forgiven.

What is a Christian conscience?

Conscience is a practical judgment concerning whether "human acts are in conformity or not with the law of God written on the heart" (*The Splendor of Truth*, #59). It is a judgment that helps us know what we must do or not do: to love and do good and to avoid evil. The judgment of conscience also assesses acts already performed. There are two key principles to keep in mind when dealing with judging right and wrong. First, we must properly form our consciences. Second, we must follow our consciences.

How do we properly form our consciences?

The duty to obey our consciences underscores the necessity of properly forming it. This is because all of us can make mistakes when we are left to ourselves. Ignorance, simply not knowing or being told the right thing to do or the wrong thing to avoid, can cause us to make false judgments. Emotions can cloud our consciences, tempting us to do things simply because they feel good. Conformity to what others are doing can also muddy our decisions.

What are the steps in conscience formation?

1. *Find the facts*. What is the issue? Who is involved? Where? When? How?

2. *Examine your motives.* Why do you want to do this?

3. *Think of the possible effects.* How will this action (or non-action) affect you? others? society as a whole? What if everyone did this?

4. *Consider alternatives.* Is there another way to act?

5. *What does the law have to say?* Law is not opposed to conscience. As a matter of fact, it greatly helps to form it. Conscience is the subjective norm or morality; law is the objective norm.

6. *What is the reasonable thing to do?* Because we are people with minds, we must use them in figuring out the right thing to do. Ask yourself what the reasonable decision is.

7. *What does your own experience and that of other people say about the issue?*

8. *What would Jesus have done?* How does this action measure up to Jesus' yardstick of love? What does the New Testament have to say? Jesus is the one perfect human response to God. Seek out his will and his example before making a decision.

9. *What is the teaching of the church?* Sincere Catholics consider it a serious obligation to consult and follow magisterial teaching on moral issues as well as to learn from competent theologians and other teachers in the church.

10. *Pray for guidance.* The Lord will help you if you ask.

11. *Admit that you sometimes sin and might be wrong.*

12. After all of this, *follow your conscience.* It is always wrong to go against your conscience.

What is sin?

Sin is a failure to love ourselves, others, and God. It is a breakdown in covenant love. Without a healthy concept of sin, people tend to see little need for Jesus, the one who frees us from sin. We talk of sin to stress the good news that God forgives us and in the person of Jesus has rescued us from its effects.

What is original sin?

Original sin refers to that condition of disharmony into which all humans are born. Universal human experience confirms the Catholic teaching that we are born into a sinful state. The evil we see around us, the anger we have within us toward others and ourselves, the good resolutions we so often break are all evidence of the sin which is part of humanity's condition.

What is personal sin?

Personal or actual sin is any free and deliberate action, word, thought, or desire which turns us away from God's law of love. It can be seen as a weakening or killing of our loving relationship with the Father. Sin breaches our baptismal mission to advance God's reign in this world, an obligation we have to God and each other.

What is venial sin?

Traditionally, venial sin refers to those acts and attitudes which fail to help us grow in our loving relationship with God or weaken the relationship. Our goal is total union with God; our direction should be one of growing closer to God each day. Venial sin involves less serious matter than mortal sin, or happens when a person does not fully reflect on or consent to what he or she is doing. All sin has social consequences; others are affected by what we do.

What is mortal sin?

Mortal sin is the harboring of a serious attitude or the commission of some serious action that kills the relationship of love between God and the sinner. In mortal sin, a person freely and consciously rejects God, God's law, and the covenant of love that God offers, preferring oneself or some created reality that is contrary to God's will.

What are the conditions for a sin to be mortal?

There are three conditions that must be met before a person sins mortally. First, the action or attitude itself must involve grave matter, for example, murder, apostasy, adultery. Second, the person must be fully aware that what he or she is doing is sinful. We are not blameworthy for something we do not know. The third condition for mortal sin is that the person must deliberately consent to the evil. Modern psychology tells us there are a number of forces and drives that limit our freedom; however, humans do have some freedom and are capable of serious and deliberate wrongdoing. Our obligation is to avoid those situations which might limit our freedom and keep us from doing the right thing.

What is the role of reconciliation?

Traditionally, we speak of a person who has turned completely away from God's love and is no longer in relationship with God as being in "the state of mortal sin." To correct this situation the sinner must repent, that is, turn back to God, admit his or her wrongdoing, and acknowledge the need for forgiveness.

Catholics celebrate the sacrament of reconciliation in which God's healing love is presented to us as a sign which reassures us of his love. The point of Jesus' parable of the Prodigal Son (Lk 15:11-31) is that no matter what we do or how often we do it, God's love is always there for us. We need but repent, that is, turn to God and accept God's love. In essence, Christian morality is saying yes to this love, letting it shine on us, and then living a life of light which shines out to others.

What is the scriptural basis for the sacrament of the anointing of the sick?

Jesus Christ is a healer. Jesus saw the hurting people in his midst and responded to them holistically—both to their bodies and spirits. Healing was a principal sign of the coming of God's kingdom. Jesus' healing ministry should be seen in the context of his forgiving sin and his proclamation of God's kingdom and the need for repentance.

Jesus charged his disciples to continue his message and mission. Thus, the early church celebrated and proclaimed the good news of salvation by continuing Jesus' healing ministry. The Letter of James provides the scriptural basis for the sacrament of anointing, the symbol of love:

> Any one of you who is ill should send for the elders of the church, and they must anoint the sick person with oil in the name of the Lord and pray over him. The prayer of faith will save the sick person and the Lord will raise him up again; and if he has committed any sins, he will be forgiven. So confess your sins to one another, and pray for one another to be cured (Jas 5:14-16).

What are the emphases in the rite?

Today, the sacrament is administered not only to the dying but also to those who are sick. The celebration of this sacrament attempts to include the prayerful support of the Christian community (the family, friends, and parish community of the sick person). It reintroduces the laying on of hands, a biblical symbol of Jesus' touch and the outpouring of the Spirit of strength, love, and forgiveness.

The rite underscores the need for the sick person to overcome the alienation caused by sickness and suffering. Today's rite also urges the person to assume a more active role, by requesting the sacrament himself or herself rather than having someone else do it. In this sense, anointing of the sick is related to the Christian vocation of witnessing; that is, the sick person witnesses to the rest of the community their total dependence on God's love and support.

What are the effects of the anointing of the sick?

Pain and suffering can make us miserable and can weaken our faith in a loving, caring God. Through this sacrament the Lord, acting through the Christian community, assures us of his care and concern. He extends his forgiveness and strengthens the sick person through spiritual healing and sometimes physical healing. Through this sacrament, the Lord invites us to integrate our sickness, even a mortal one, into the mystery of his own suffering, death, and resurrection—the paschal mystery that has won for us eternal salvation. The sacrament reminds the community, too, that it must stand by and love its Christian brothers and sisters in times of need.

How is the anointing of the sick celebrated?

Typically the sacrament of the anointing of the sick is celebrated individually during a serious illness or before a serious operation. If possible, family and friends should be present. There is a growing trend toward celebration of the sacrament within the context of the eucharist.

The rite itself begins with a greeting, a sprinkling with holy water, a penitential rite, and the liturgy of the word which recalls the Lord's healing power. All present then join in a litany of prayers for the sick. After the priest lays his hands on the person to be anointed, he blesses the oil and then anoints the forehead and hands. He prays:

Through this holy anointing may the Lord in his love and mercy help you with the grace of the Holy Spirit. Amen. May the Lord who frees you from sin save you and raise you up. Amen.

A prayer after the anointing and the Lord's Prayer follow. Holy communion may then be given before the final blessing which concludes the service.

16

CHRISTIAN MARRIAGE
The Sacrament of Friendship

All sacraments are signs of God's friendship and love; they are celebrations of his ongoing presence to us in our ordinary lives. Christian marriage, celebrated in the sacrament of matrimony, is truly the sacrament of friendship. Christians who marry in the Lord are a living sign of God's love in human relationships, in friendship, in life-giving procreation, in family living.

What is the sacrament of marriage?

In the sacrament of matrimony a baptized man and woman vow their love in an exclusive, permanent, sexual partnership. This union is marked by love, respect, care and concern, and a commitment to share responsibility in the raising of a family if God should bless them with children.

Christian marriage is an extraordinary sign of God working through and in the ordinary. A good marriage is a holy covenant involving three persons. The couple is joined on their life's journey by Jesus Christ who promises to bless, sustain, and rejoice in their union.

In the covenant of Christian marriage, a husband and wife freely bind themselves together for life. Theirs is a commitment to love exclusively.

What do the Hebrew scriptures reveal about marriage?

In the book of Genesis, God revealed to the Jewish people two profound truths about the *purposes* of marriage. First, marriage is a share in God's creative act of bringing new life into the world. Second, marriage is meant to enhance, celebrate, and increase the love between the wife and husband. Genesis tells us that God established marriage and sex and declared that they are good.

What does the New Testament reveal about marriage?

The New Testament reveals further important insights into the nature of marriage. Jesus' attendance at the wedding feast of Cana implicitly underscores the goodness and naturalness of marriage. When Jesus explicitly teaches about marriage, he reaffirms the original intention of his Father—that marriage should be a permanent, exclusive love relationship:

> "Everyone who divorces his wife and marries another is guilty of adultery, and the man who marries a woman divorced by her husband commits adultery" (Lk 16:18).

The union of a husband and wife is like the union of Christ with his church. Marriage is a covenant, a total lifelong commitment that mirrors Christ's love for his church.

What is the proximate preparation for a Christian marriage?

Preparation for a Christian marriage in most dioceses includes a policy that the engaged couple attend pre-marriage conferences. These church-sponsored classes give the couple an opportunity to learn about the sacramental commitment from a priest and learn many practical details about married life from couples who are living the sacrament, as well as from a doctor and other experts on marriage. Topics examined include love and communication, the raising of a family, the role of a faith life in marriage, and the plans for the actual ceremony.

What are the requirements for a valid marriage?

To celebrate the sacrament of marriage validly, the couple must be of mature age, unmarried, not closely related by blood or marriage, and freely desire to marry. They must intend to commit themselves to a lifelong covenant of love. Furthermore, they must be capable of sharing sexually since sexual intercourse is a sign of mutual love and union, the full expression of the mutual love between husband and wife. Finally, the couple must be open to the possibility of raising a family if God blesses the marriage with children.

How is the sacrament of marriage celebrated?

Ordinarily Christian marriage takes place during a eucharistic celebration. The spouses, ministers of Christ's grace, confer the sacrament of marriage on each other. They express their consent—the indispensable element that brings marriage into being—by exchanging vows in the presence of the priest, two witnesses, and the assembled Christian community. The traditional words used are:

I, (name),
take you, (name),
to be my wife/husband.
I promise to be true to you
in good times and in bad,
in sickness and in health.
I will love you and honor you
all the days of my life.

As the church's official witness, the priest blesses the rings and asks the couple to exchange them as symbols of fidelity and unending love.

The celebration of the wedding ceremony is only one important element in the sacrament. The sacrament of marriage unfolds over the years as the husband and wife live out their mutual relationship with each other and the Lord. The risen Lord promises to be with the couple to sustain them on their life journey.

> The sacrament of matrimony ... gives spouses the grace to love each other with the love with which Christ has loved his Church; the grace of the sacrament thus perfects the human love of the spouses, strengthens their indissoluble unity and sanctifies them on the way to eternal life (*CCC*, #1661).

Why is Christian marriage forever?

Christian marriage is a permanent commitment because it is a prime way to bring Christ into the world and pass on the Christian faith. This is certainly true for the children who result from the marriage. They need the stable, reassuring love of a solid marriage to develop healthy attitudes to life and to God.

But a faithful marriage is a powerful sign to others as well. The Christian husband and wife point to the mystery of God's love at work in ordinary life. Their fidelity and exclusive love is an extraordinary sign to the world of God's fidelity and undying love for his people.

Jesus himself underscored the permanence of the marriage bond:

> Have you not read that the Creator from the beginning *made them male and female* and that he said: *This is why a man leaves his father and mother and becomes attached to his wife, and the two become*

one flesh? They are no longer two, therefore, but one flesh. So then, what God has united, human beings must not divide (Mt 19:4-6).

The covenant made between two validly married Catholics can only be dissolved by the death of one of the partners. In extraordinary circumstances a couple may separate for the good of the children and the individuals involved. Though the civil authority may dissolve the legal aspects of a valid marriage (called in civil law a divorce), the state has no authority to dissolve a true Christian marriage—its true sacramental nature.

Christ calls his disciples to high standards. The church encourages a person who is suffering from a broken marriage to continue to celebrate the sacraments and remain close to the Christian community. The Lord promises in a special way to bless those who suffer most. Fellow Christians should support hurting brothers and sisters and pray for them.

What is an annulment?

An annulment is an official declaration of the church that what appeared to be a valid Christian marriage in fact was not. A couple may have been psychologically immature when they entered the marriage, or lacking true understanding of the demands a marriage covenant makes. One or both partners might not have given free, true consent to the marriage. Perhaps one or both partners intended never to have children. Possibly one or both partners were incapable of sexual relations.

A "failed" marriage may never have been a true Christian marriage to begin with. In these cases the couple should submit their situation to the diocesan marriage tribunal (court) for examination and judgment. If it can be shown that the marriage was not valid from the beginning, then the individuals involved are free to enter a true Christian marriage in the future.

What does the church teach about sexual sharing?

The Catholic community praises married love as a great gift from God. Sexual intercourse is a profound means of love and commitment between a man and a woman. Its purpose in God's plan is twofold: *unitive*, that is, to bond a man and woman together as partners for life; and *procreative*, that is, to share in God's creative activity of bringing new life into the world.

As a deep symbol of love between a man and a woman, sexual intercourse (and all acts leading up to it) expresses a total, unreserved commitment of love. The church believes this can take place only when a couple has declared lifelong devotion to each other, that is, in a marriage.

What does the church teach about adultery?

Sexual intimacy signifies a total giving and a total receiving. To engage in sexual relations outside of marriage is to misuse this profound sign of human love. Thus adultery—sexual intimacy engaged in by a married person with another who is not his or her spouse—is a serious breach in the covenant love of Christian marriage. Adultery is a failure to honor the fundamental commitment of marriage; it threatens the very stability of the family.

What does the church teach about fornication?

Fornication is sexual intercourse engaged in by unmarried people. It is also wrong because it often exploits others or is indulged in for selfish motives under the guise of love. God intended intimate sexual sharing to express total love and commitment; that kind of love and commitment exists only within the context of marriage.

What does the church teach about masturbation?

The church also teaches that masturbation—self-induced sexual pleasure—is wrong because it misuses the powers of sex which in God's plan are directed to sexual intimacy with another and with bringing new life into the world.

What does the church teach about homosexuality?

The church distinguishes between a homosexual *condition* and homosexual *acts*. Homosexuality as a condition exists when a person's sexual desires are directed to a member of the same sex rather than to a member of the opposite sex. People with homosexual tendencies do not choose their homosexual condition, which is a trial for most of them. They deserve respect, compassion, and sensitivity. And unjust discrimination toward them is un-Christian. However, the church teaches that homosexual *acts* are intrinsically disordered and against the natural law. They are a serious violation of God's plan for male/female bonding and are not open to the procreation of life. They can never be approved.

What does the church teach about family planning?

Birth control refers to a couple's deliberate limitation of the number of children they will bring into the world. Christian parents are called upon to plan the size of their families in a responsible way. Physical and psychological health, family finances, the population explosion, and the current number of children are some of the factors which will help a husband and wife determine the size of their family. The church teaches that for a *legitimate* reason a Catholic couple has the right and duty to practice natural methods of birth control.

What is natural birth control?

Periodic abstinence from sexual relations and natural family planning methods are moral means of birth control because they work in harmony with normal, natural bodily functions. The *Family Life Bureau* of most dioceses sponsors classes to help train couples in these methods.

What does the church teach about artificial birth control?

Church teaching holds that artificial means of contraception are contrary to God's will. This teaching rests on the Catholic view that marriage is directed to two aims simultaneously: the procreation (and rearing) of children, and the mutual love and affection of the couple. Official church teaching maintains that any artificial means used to frustrate the natural processes of procreation goes against the very nature of marriage.

In striving to live the ideal, sometimes people fall short. The bishops advise us not to judge the consciences of those couples who fall short of the church's teaching. This moral judgment is God's to make. Couples must follow their consciences in this moral issue and all moral issues.

17

CHRISTIAN MINISTRY
Christian Service and Holy Orders

A Christian is a disciple. Disciples learn from and strive to imitate their master. Christian disciples want to be like Jesus. To be like Jesus means simply to serve others in imitation of him.

What is ministry?

The common vocation of all Christians is to minister, that is, to serve others in the name of Christ. Minister means "one who serves." Christian ministry means serving others in Christ and because of Christ.

Is every Christian a minister?

Through baptism and confirmation, every member of the church is called to serve others in imitation of Jesus. This service vocation is the universal vocation of all disciples. Jesus empowers us for ministry by sending us the Holy Spirit who showers on us the gifts necessary to do God's work.

What are some ways to minister?

In general, ministry involves many different ways to serve others. The obligation of every baptized Christian is to bring Christian values to everyday life. In his social justice teachings, John Paul II has reminded all Christians of their need to identify in solidarity with the poor. The laity, in particular, have a pre-eminent role in serving the cause of peace and justice in their ordinary life.

Besides serving others in the world, Catholics can serve fellow members of the church in many ways.

For example, the ordained ministries of bishop, presbyter (priest), and deacon are essential church ministries for the care of God's people and for the faithful celebration of the sacraments. Also, the following list includes some of the key opportunities for lay ministry which the Holy Spirit in our day is inviting God's people to undertake:

- Religious educators, catechists, and teachers
- Eucharistic ministers, lectors, music and art ministers, hospitality ministers
- Ministers to the sick and handicapped
- Parish councilors and financial consultants
- Ministers to the separated and divorced
- Ministers to the poor

What is the ordained ministry?

Ordained ministers serve in one of the structured ministries of the church; they are entrusted with leading the church through a special ministry of service to the Christian community and by extension to the whole world. Ordained ministers include bishops, presbyters (priests), and deacons. Their special role is to proclaim God's word to all people, to lead the Christian community in worship, and to model in a special way the universal Christian vocation of service.

What is holy orders?

Holy orders can be described as the sacrament of Christian ministry. Through the laying on of hands by bishops and a prayer of consecration, the sacrament of holy orders confers on certain men a special role of service within the Christian community. Holy orders deepens the life of Jesus in the ordained men called to serve him. And the sacrament also gives actual graces, divine help, to provide the wisdom and fortitude to live the life of an ordained minister. Finally, the church teaches that holy orders—like baptism and confirmation—imparts a sacramental "character" that permanently marks the ordained man as a deacon, priest, or bishop—a living sign who points to the Lord and his coming.

What is the role of ministerial priesthood today?

Ministerial priesthood is often seen in terms of the images of prophet, priest, and king—roles fulfilled by Jesus. Ordained ministers have the special vocation to proclaim God's word (prophet), build up and lead the priestly people in worship (priest), and imitate Christ's servanthood by serving God's people and acting as a sign of Christ in the world (king).

The ministerial priesthood has the task not only of representing Christ—Head of the Church—before the assembly of the faithful, but also of acting in the name of the whole church when presenting to God the prayer of the church, and above all when offering the Eucharistic sacrifice (*CCC,* #1552).

What are the functions of the bishops, priests, and deacons?

The ordained ministries are those of bishop, priest, and deacon. Traditionally the bishop is the successor of the apostles. He is the overseer of the local church community and a symbol of church unity. His consecration confers on him the fullness of the sacrament of holy orders: the offices of teaching, governing, and sanctifying. The chief responsibilities of bishops are to preach the gospel, to see to the administration of the sacraments, and to serve the needy in his diocese.

Bishops ordain priests to help them carry out their duties of preaching the gospel, shepherding the faithful, and celebrating divine worship.

Deacons cooperate with the bishop and priests in liturgical celebrations, in the distribution of communion, in preaching the gospel, in baptizing, in witnessing and blessing marriages, in presiding at funerals, and in the social work of the church.

How is holy orders celebrated?

The sacrament of holy orders can be celebrated in three ways: in the ordination of a bishop, priest, or deacon. Ordination is celebrated within a eucharist presided over by a bishop or bishops. God's people, from whom an ordained minister is called in order to serve the Christian community and all people everywhere, are present at this celebration.

At the ordination of priests, candidates are called forth by name after the liturgy of the word. The bishop questions them about their willingness to share in his care for God's people—in celebrating the sacraments, in preaching God's word, and in a life dedicated to God's reign. The visible sign of ordination is the laying on of hands by the bishop who recites a prayer of consecration that asks God for the outpouring of the Holy Spirit and gifts for the priestly ministry.

The hands of the newly ordained priests are anointed and the symbols of their office are conferred (vestments, a chalice containing water and wine, and a paten on which rests the bread to be consecrated). The sign of peace is exchanged. The liturgy continues with the newly ordained concelebrating with the bishop and their fellow priests.

What are the reasons for a celibate clergy?

Church law requires priests and bishops of the Roman Catholic church not to marry. This is known as celibacy. Priests undertake this discipline freely to express their wholehearted commitment in serving both God and his people. The following four reasons are generally offered for this practice.

Celibacy gives a person more freedom to serve Christ. Second, giving up a family is a concrete witness to the sacrifices in the name of the gospel asked by Jesus of some of his followers. Third, and perhaps most important, by living as a loving celibate person, a priest is in reality pointing to eternal life when there will be no marriage. Finally, there is the witness of Jesus himself who did not marry so that he could be totally involved in doing God's will in serving others.

What is a religious vocation?

Vocation means "calling," an invitation by the Lord to a special kind of service. One can be called to serve God as a married person, in the single life, as a priest, or in religious life.

Down through the centuries certain Christian men (religious brothers or priests belonging to a religious community) and women (religious sisters or nuns) have consecrated themselves to God and the work of God's kingdom by taking vows of poverty, chastity, and obedience. By taking the vow of poverty, those living the religious life are attempting to free themselves of the things of this world so that they can be attached to the One who is really important, Jesus Christ. By vowing chastity for the sake of the gospel, religious become a sign to the world that they belong simultaneously to Christ and to all people. Through the vow of obedience, religious commit themselves to serve their religious community, which in turn is dedicated to serving the Christian community. All three vows are positive ways to liberate those living them to a more active life of prayer and service in God's church.

18

PRAYER

We who follow the Lord are called to holiness, that is, to true union with God in both mind and heart. Growth in holiness is a gift from God. The Holy Spirit never forces God's love on us, but empowers us to respond freely to the opportunities God gives us. Prayer is an essential way to get closer to God. Catholic tradition offers many different ways to pray, many different paths to our Lord.

What is prayer?

A traditional Catholic definition of prayer is "the lifting of one's mind and heart to God." A popular description states that prayer is "loving conversation with God." The great spiritual writer Thomas Merton defined prayer as "the consciousness of one's union with God, an awareness of one's inner self."

However we define prayer, there is always a dimension of turning to God and becoming aware of God's presence. When we pray we are awake to the marvelous activity of God in our lives.

What are the purposes of prayer?

One way to distinguish among the different kinds of prayer is through the acronym ACTS, which helps us remember the four purposes of prayer: Adoration, Contrition, Thanksgiving and Supplication. We pray to adore God as the source of all blessings and to praise God as gracious, loving, and saving. We express sorrow to God for the sins we have committed when we offer prayers of contrition. We thank God for the many gifts God has given to us. Finally, prayers of supplication, or petition, are requests for God's help. A special form of petition is intercessory prayer which asks God's help on behalf of other people, a special way to show love and mercy.

How do public and private prayers differ?

In the public prayer of the church—and the liturgy is the prime example—Christians come and pray together as members of Christ's family to praise God, seek forgiveness, ask for help, or offer thanks.

Private prayer is engaged in by an individual Christian in personal communication with God. Private prayer, though, can certainly be for others; we can and should pray for our families, friends, and members of the church, for leaders, for people in need, for our enemies, indeed for all people.

How do formal and spontaneous prayers differ?

When we recite the Hail Mary or read the psalms aloud, we are engaging in formal vocal prayer; we are using prayers already composed according to a certain form. But we are not limited to saying formal prayers. Our prayer can also be spontaneous, that is, in our own words and following no set formula.

What are the basics of prayer?

To grow in friendship with the Lord requires time. It is good to remember the following.

Place/Time. You can pray anywhere, but it is good to find a special place where you can slow down, relax, and focus your attention. You can also pray at any time, but it is a good idea to select a regular time each day. Prayer is a habit. We learn to pray by praying.

Relaxation. Prayer demands our attention. Masters of the spiritual life suggest that we assume a body position that keeps us alert but also helps us relax. We should also spend some time calming our bodies so that our minds and spirits are free to commune with the Lord.

Proper Attitude. Prayer requires openness and devotion to God. It is always good to begin our prayer by recalling God's presence and friendship and the many gifts God has bestowed on us.

How can we develop a positive attitude toward prayer?

Remember that God is *Abba*. Our God is a loving Father. We need never fear approaching him. God knows our needs and is vitally concerned with our lives. We can trust our Father.

Be persistent. Jesus taught that we should "pray continually and never lose heart."

Be confident. Deep faith in God should accompany our persistence in prayer.

Be humble. Jesus instructed his disciples to pray simply and humbly. He also taught us there is no need to heap up a lot of words because our heavenly Father already knows our needs. Humility is a true sign of our love for God.

Be forgiving. The God of forgiveness wants us to approach him with forgiveness in our hearts. This is a sign of sincerity and peace that will help make our prayer beneficial for us.

What is vocal prayer?

Vocal prayers are usually said aloud and with others, for example, at Mass. They can either follow a prescribed formula or be spontaneous. Vocal prayers can also be "one-liners," for example, "Holy Spirit, enlighten me" or "Jesus, help me."

Some prayers are so familiar to us that we forget to reflect on what we are saying. To counteract this tendency, it is helpful to pause before praying, recall God's presence and the reason why we are praying, and then consciously reflect on the prayer.

What is special about the Lord's Prayer?

Jesus, a model pray-er, taught us the Lord's Prayer which serves as a pattern for Christian prayer. As the church father Tertullian observed, it summarizes the whole gospel.

- In the Lord's Prayer we address God as *Abba*, who has adopted us into the divine family and who reveals that we are related to all other humans. We are God's people.
- We acknowledge God's majesty and mysterious presence in heaven and in the hearts of the just.
- We pray that everyone will acknowledge God's holiness, and we commit ourselves to "hallowing" God's name by living in God's love.
- We pray for the full coming of God's reign. In doing so, we join Jesus in his work of spreading God's peace and justice, truth and service, especially to the needy.
- We petition God to give us our daily bread: what we need for physical life—food, shelter, clothing; psychological life—friendship, love, and companionship; and spiritual life—the eucharistic Jesus.
- We humbly ask God to forgive us our sins. And we pledge that we will forgive others as we have been forgiven.
- We petition God not to allow us to take the path that leads to sin. We ask God to strengthen us to persevere to the end of our days by avoiding the snares of Satan and a sensuous, materialistic, and violent society that ignores God and tempts us to rely solely on ourselves.

How do we pray with scripture?

Christians from the earliest centuries have found reading and reflecting on the Bible as the living word of God a most helpful means to spiritual growth.

To read the Bible prayerfully, select a passage, find a quiet place, and recall the presence of God within your heart and in God's written word. Ask the Lord to help you see that what you are to read is his personal word spoken directly to you. Begin reading slowly and reflectively, pausing frequently to see what the text is saying and what meaning it might have for your life. While reading, turn frequently to the Lord and speak to him as to a friend, asking him to make his word take root in your life. After your period of prayer, think back over what you learned and take a key insight with you. Thank the Lord for what he has given you. Then, throughout the day, return to the insight you gained as a way of remembering the Lord's gift to you.

What is meditation?

In our day, meditation has grown in popularity; but for centuries the church has had a rich tradition of both meditation and contemplation.

Meditation is "tuning into God," thinking about God and trying to become aware of God's presence in our lives. It usually involves active use of the mind and imagination. There are many methods of meditation. All of them, though, suggest the following:

1. Find a quiet place to pray, a place where you will not be disturbed.

2. Quiet your body. Relax your body so your mind can focus on the meditation.

3. Now direct your attention to some object of meditation. You may focus on a crucifix, or recall how the Lord met you through other people during the

course of your day, or read a passage from the New Testament.

4. Pause periodically to talk intimately to the Lord.

5. At the end of your prayer time, thank the Lord for his friendship and any spiritual insights he might have given you. Make a resolution to do something with your insights and return to them periodically throughout the day.

What is contemplation?

Contemplation, sometimes known as "mental prayer," is more passive than meditation. A person doesn't really try to think about anything. Rather, the pray-er puts himself or herself in God's presence and simply enjoys God's loving company. Contemplation is wordless prayer. Contemplation is a way of praying which leaves behind images and words in order to meet the living God who is beyond human comprehension and understanding.

What is the "Jesus Prayer"?

The Jesus Prayer consists of the words, "Lord Jesus Christ, Son of God, have mercy on me, a sinner." Alternative forms are "Jesus, have mercy on me" or, simply, "Jesus." Rhythmic breathing is often used when reciting this prayer.

How does praying affect us?

Praying on a regular basis keeps our true goal in life before us. It helps us become more aware of God's presence and realize God's deep love for us as individuals. This awareness helps make us more loving and patient and attuned to what is really important.

19

The Communion of Saints
and
Our Blessed Mother

The Acts of the Apostles and the epistles com-
monly refer to Christians as "the saints." The claim
being made was not that Christians were already
perfect. Rather, the early church writings called
Christians saints because the Lord calls us to holiness—the word saint means "holy one." Through our
baptismal initiation into Jesus' own life of holiness,
Christians have been given a privileged vocation: to
become saints in imitation of our Lord.

Who belongs to the communion of saints?

The communion of saints, that is, the communion
of the holy, includes all those who are now living on
earth (the pilgrim church), those who are being
purified in purgatory (the church suffering), and
those who are blessed in heaven (the church in glory).

The term communion of saints also underscores
that the People of God, the church, is a eucharistic
community. The church is a community of people, a
real communion, gathered around the eucharistic
table of the risen Lord. Through the power of the
Holy Spirit, the church is united into a communion
of love and holiness as it partakes of the gift of the
risen Lord, the source of all holiness.

**What is the basis for belief in the communion
of saints?**

The doctrine of the communion of saints flows
from our belief that we Christians are closely united
in the Spirit of Jesus Christ. The bond of love makes

us one. Those of us who are still living depend on the prayers and good works of our Christian brothers and sisters who are united to us in the friendship of the Lord. We also believe in the value of prayer for our departed brothers and sisters who are being purified in purgatory. Finally, we believe that those Christian heroes whom we call saints in heaven are vitally interested in those of us who are still living.

Who is a saint?

A saint is a good person. Saints are people who always choose the better of two courses open to them. Saints are Christian models of holiness.

Under the guidance of the Holy Spirit the Catholic church will sometimes declare that a person who lived a good life and died a death joined to Jesus is a saint. The process leading to adding a person's name to the list of saints (canonization) involves a careful study of that person's life and a sign from God (usually miracles performed in that person's name) that this person is truly a saint and worthy of our imitation.

Every person in heaven is truly a saint, whether canonized or not. Some of these saints may be our own deceased friends and relatives.

Why do we pray to the saints?

Devotion to the saints is a traditional means to holiness. We do not pray to the saints as though they were God. Rather, we petition them to intercede for us with our heavenly Father. They are living a deep, personal, and loving relationship with God; they have proven their friendship by the extraordinary goodness of their lives while on earth. We pray to the saints, especially those to whom we feel particularly close, to befriend us, too. We ask these personal heroes to take our petitions to God on our behalf.

What is Mary's role in the church?

Mary, foremost among the saints, has a special place in the story of salvation history. The New Testament reports that she was singled out and graced by God for the special and unique privilege of being the mother of the Savior. When Jesus launched his public ministry, Mary faithfully witnessed and supported him. With courage and sorrow in her heart, she stood at the foot of the cross in Jesus' dying moments. Finally, the Bible tells us that Mary was with the apostles praying in the upper room after Jesus' resurrection, expectantly awaiting the descent of the Holy Spirit. The church teaches that Mary is the greatest Christian saint of all, the perfect model of Christian faith.

What are some of Mary's titles?

The church honors Mary with many titles such as Our Lady, Mother of God, Our Lady of the Immaculate Conception, Blessed Mother, Mother of the Church, Ever Virgin, Queen of Heaven and Earth. These titles reflect what the church believes and teaches about her.

What do we mean by the Immaculate Conception?

The church teaches that Mary was conceived without original sin. This means that from the first moment of her existence Mary was full of grace, that is, free of any alienation from God caused by original sin. Because of Mary's special role in God's saving plan, she was graced with this divine favor in anticipation of her son's death and resurrection.

What is the church's teaching about Mary's virginity?

The Apostles' Creed states that Jesus was conceived by the Holy Spirit and born of the virgin Mary.

Mary conceived Jesus without a human father, and the church has traditionally taught that she was a virgin "before, in, and after" the birth of the Lord.

How is Mary the Mother of God and the Mother of the Church?

At the Council of Ephesus (A.D. 431) the church solemnly taught that Mary is *theotokos*, that is, "bearer of God." By being the mother of Jesus, Mary is truly the mother of God. It is most appropriate for Christians to address Mary with the lofty title: Mother of God.

But Mary is also our mother, the Mother of the Church. By giving Mary to us as our mother, the Lord wishes the church to learn what God does for those he loves. The church also has a maternal role. As such she can learn much from Mary, the perfect model of faith, obedience, fidelity, compassion, and prayerfulness. Mary is the model of Christian holiness and an image of God's love for his people.

What is the Assumption?

In 1950 Pope Pius XII officially proclaimed the doctrine of the assumption: "The Immaculate Mother of God, the ever Virgin Mary, having completed the course of her earthly life, was assumed body and soul into heavenly glory." In her assumption, Mary was preserved from the decay of death. Mary, the mother of the Savior, has a unique share in the Lord's resurrection.

Why do Catholics have special veneration for Mary?

Catholics venerate Mary because she is the Mother of God and our mother. By praying to and honoring Mary in a special way, we are led to love her and to imitate her many virtues, especially her total commitment to God's will and her single-hearted faith in God's work.

Sometimes Catholics are accused of worshipping Mary as though she were a god. True devotion to Mary honors Mary; God alone may be worshipped. When we pray in Mary's honor, we are really thanking and praising God for blessing one of our sisters.

What is the Rosary?

The Rosary is a perfect blend of vocal prayers and meditation. The vocal prayers center on the recitation of a number of decades of Hail Marys, each decade introduced by the Lord's Prayer and concluded by a Glory Be. During the recitation of these vocal prayers, we meditate on certain events, or mysteries, from the life of Christ and Mary. The repetition of the Hail Marys helps to keep our minds from distractions as we meditate on the mysteries. These mysteries are divided into the following three categories:

Joyful Mysteries
1. The Annunciation
2. The Visitation of Mary to Elizabeth
3. The Birth of Jesus
4. The Presentation of Jesus in the Temple
5. The Finding of Jesus in the Temple

Sorrowful Mysteries
1. The Agony in the Garden
2. The Scourging at the Pillar
3. The Crowning with Thorns
4. The Carrying of the Cross
5. The Crucifixion

Glorious Mysteries
1. The Resurrection
2. The Ascension
3. The Descent of the Holy Spirit on the Apostles
4. The Assumption of Mary into Heaven
5. The Crowning of Mary Queen of Heaven

20

CHRISTIAN DESTINY
The Last Things

One apparent defeat that stares all humans directly in the face is death. It is inevitable. But death does not have the last word; life does. The good news of Christianity is that life is never really over. Jesus taught:

"I am the resurrection.
Anyone who believes in me, even though that
    person dies, will live,
and whoever lives and believes in me
will never die" (Jn 11:25-26).

What does our faith teach us about death and judgment?

As a result of original sin, people must suffer "bodily death, from which they would have been preserved had they not sinned" [*Church in the Modern World* #18], (CCC, #1018).

The book of Ecclesiastes teaches that it is natural to die: "There is a season for everything. ... A time for giving birth, a time for dying" (Eccl 3:1-2). To make sense out of death and our own personal future death, we must look to Jesus Christ.

Death is a great mystery. But Christian faith reveals that Jesus Christ, our Savior, has conquered death. Jesus Christ lives. Jesus Christ wants us to befriend him in this life so that we can live joyfully with him in eternity. This is not only the good news of the gospel, this is the greatest news humanity is privileged to know.

In *Dictionary of the Bible* John McKenzie writes, "For each [person] the 'day of judgment' is the day on which he [she] makes a permanent decision to accept Jesus Christ or to reject him." This is known as the *particular judgment*. But McKenzie also notes that the Bible reveals there is to be another judgment at the end of time, a *general* or *last judgment* where there is final victory over evil. As the Apostles' Creed puts it, "Jesus shall come to judge the living and the dead."

What is the particular judgment?

The church teaches that each individual will immediately appear before God after death for a *particular judgment*. The particular judgment will reveal us for who we truly are. After death each of us will see his or her life as God sees it: a loving response to God or a self-centered turning away from God's love.

The Father of Jesus—our Father—is not a cruel, vindictive God. At the particular judgment God will judge us lovingly, mercifully, and justly. God's judgment will simply be a declaration of what is the truth about our acceptance or rejection of God.

What is the general or last judgment?

The general judgment is the time at which God will establish the heavenly community. It will be preceded by the resurrection of the dead. At that time, the entire saving plan of God will be evident to everyone who ever lived. Jesus will serve as judge. His goodness, justice, mercy, and peace will establish God's reign in all its glory. People will recognize the sealing of their own destinies and their relationship to others. All will acknowledge and marvel at the majesty of the Lord.

The Last Judgment will come when Christ returns in glory. ... The Last Judgment will reveal that God's justice triumphs over all the injustices committed by his creatures and that God's love is stronger than death (CCC, #1040).

What is the second coming of Christ?

Christians believe that God's reign is here in our midst, but it has not yet been fully established on earth. All Christians look for the future day when Christ's work will be complete. The day of this glorious future will be the day when human history will come to a definite close, the day when Jesus Christ will come again. On this day the reign of God in all its eternal glory will be finally established.

When will Christ's second coming take place?

We do not know when the world will end and Jesus will come again in glory. The gospels (for example, Mark 13, Luke 21, and Matthew 24—25) and the book of Revelation use a special symbolic language, *apocalyptic language*, when writing about the end of the world and Jesus' second coming. This language should not be interpreted in a literal manner. Christians look forward to this day as a joyful encounter with the risen Lord, as a time when eternity and its promises of perfect happiness, joy, and peace will be fulfilled.

What the church believes and teaches about the end of the world is that human history will come to a close at some time in the future. Jesus will come again at the *parousia*, a word which means "presence" or "arrival." When this takes place, at a time known to God alone, everyone who ever lived will recognize Jesus as Lord of all.

What do we believe about the resurrection of the body?

The resurrection of the body means that each person will be completely human—body and soul—

for all eternity, sharing in the glorious life of our Lord Jesus Christ. St. Paul tells us that our resurrected bodies will be immortal, imperishable, glorious, powerful, and spiritual.

What is heaven?

Heaven is the state of eternal life in union with God and all those who share in his life. In heaven we will be given the "beatific vision," we will "see" God as God really is, and this seeing will bring us happiness. God made us to share the divine life; God made us for eternal happiness. Heaven is the final, perfect human fulfillment, that state of being that makes us wholly what we are meant to be, that state which will make us happy.

What is purgatory?

The church teaches that purgatory, a place or state of purification, exists as a preparation for entrance into heaven. The church encourages us to pray, give alms, and do works of penance on behalf of those in purgatory.

Purgatory means "purification, cleansing." What we need cleansing of is any venial sin or any punishment due our sin which is present at death. In one sense, for the Christian the process of purification takes place each day as we live and attempt to rid ourselves of sin and attachment to self.

The exact nature of purgatory has never been defined by the church. The church has never officially declared what kind of "place" purgatory is or "how long it lasts." Some theologians suggest that when we see Christ's loving look, our own sinful infidelities "burn" us to the degree that we have failed to respond to God's love. This encounter burns away imperfections and opens the person totally to God.

What is hell?

Hell is eternal separation from God. In the New Testament Jesus clearly stated its existence in a number of places.

The church teaches that there is a hell, but that the images employed by scripture to describe it are symbolic. They are attempts to describe the horror of an eternal life alienated from God and his love. This alienation extends to all interpersonal relationships. The person who dies having turned away freely and deliberately from God's redeeming love has chosen to live a life turned in on self—eternally.

Who is in hell?

We know that it is possible to choose self over God and thus merit eternal punishment. But we simply do not know who—in the depths of their consciences—have definitively rejected God.

The person who loves God and translates that love into actions need not obsessively fear hell. Those who love God know that God is not out to get us. God respects our freedom, even if we sin. But we should never forget that he is a God of both mercy *and* justice.

Hell's principal punishment consists of eternal separation from God in whom alone man can have the life and happiness for which he was created and for which he longs (*CCC*, #1057).

21

ECUMENISM
The Church and
Other Religions

Catholicism is the largest Christian denomination in the world and the largest branch of any of the world religions. We must be aware, however, that most of the world's population is not Catholic. Millions of people belong to other religions. Yet they are our brothers and sisters too. Today the church's attitude is one of profound respect and reverence toward other religions and those who practice them. Christians and Catholics can and should gain much nourishment from respecting and learning about other religious traditions.

What are the major world religions?

The major world religions are typically divided into the religions of the West and the religions of the East. The religions of the West include Judaism and its two spiritual descendants: Christianity and Islam. Judaism defines itself as a people of the covenant: Yahweh formed and sustained the Jewish people in return for their love and worship. Yahweh is their God, and Israel is God's people. Christianity professes that Jesus of Nazareth, a Jewish carpenter and teacher, is the Messiah, God's own Son, who fulfills all the promises made to Israel. The Moslems share with Judaism and Christianity a strong faith in one God. Though Islam acknowledges Jesus as a prophet and honors Mary his mother, it maintains that Mohammed is Allah's greatest prophet.

The religions of the East include Hinduism and Buddhism which were born on the Indian subcontinent, Taoism in China, and the Shinto religions in Japan.

To these major religions we could add numerous other religions, including the religions of the American Indians and various aboriginal people, for example, of Australia and Africa.

What are the major Christian religions?

Christianity is numerically the largest major world religion. It is divided into three major sections: Catholic, Orthodox, and Protestant.

Catholicism, the largest Christian denomination, includes those Christians who acknowledge the primacy of the pope.

The Eastern Orthodox (or Orthodox) are those churches (notably the Greek and Russian Orthodox churches) that are historically separated from Rome, that is, not in union with the pope. Of all Christian groups, the Orthodox are closest to Roman Catholicism in faith, theology, and church structures.

The Reformation of the sixteenth century resulted in the formation of the mainstream Protestant churches. These denominations share many beliefs in common with Catholics, notably the articles of faith in the Nicene Creed, but they differ on other points of belief and practice.

What is ecumenism?

Ours is an age of ecumenism. *Ecumenism* comes from a Greek word which means "universal." The ecumenical movement generally means two things: 1) It refers to the attempt among all world religions to understand one another better and to overcome needless opposition, and 2) when applied to Christians, the ecumenical movement refers to the efforts of Christian denominations to work for greater unity among themselves and to better understand and improve relations with the other major world religions.

The Catholic church did not officially participate in non-Catholic ecumenical efforts until the Second Vatican Council (1962-1965). The *Decree on Ecumenism* made efforts for Christian unity a top priority for the church and praised efforts on behalf of ecumenism.

Does ecumenism mean that all churches are the same?

Work on behalf of ecumenism does not mean that the church denies its unique role in God's plan of salvation. For example, the church still teaches that the fullness of the truth and grace of Jesus Christ subsists (can be found) in the Roman Catholic church. Nevertheless, the church also teaches that the Holy Spirit works in all people of good will in order to build up God's kingdom. Other churches share in the building up of the kingdom to the degree that they are related to the one true church of Jesus Christ.

What is the goal of ecumenism?

The goal of Christian ecumenism is a common commitment among Christians to live out the gospel and to be open to the unifying action of the Holy Spirit.

How can the individual Christian work toward Christian unity?

A primary duty of Catholics in the work for unity is to make sure that the Catholic church itself is living the gospel message in fidelity to Jesus Christ. Furthermore, Catholics can acknowledge the spiritual gifts which our Lord has endowed on our Christian brothers and sisters and remember that their faith, hope, and love can inspire us. In addition, we can do the following:

Prayer. We can pray *for* Christian unity, asking the Spirit to guide our efforts, and *with* our Christian brothers and sisters.

Study. We have a duty to know better the depths of our own faith and to appreciate the meaning of church doctrines so that we can help others to understand them as well. Knowledge of other religions can also be very helpful for mutual understanding.

Communication. As individuals we can share our own Catholic beliefs and engage in open exchanges with members of other faiths as occasions arise. We can share points of view in Christian harmony, charitably and with understanding. The Second Vatican Council encourages us to eliminate prejudicial language from our conversation.

Cooperation. The church calls on us to work together with our Christian brothers and sisters of other communions on projects of social action. Putting the gospel into action in joint efforts of Christian charity can go a long way in bringing Christians together.

22

BEING CATHOLIC
Summary

As we conclude our study of Catholicism, let us never forget that to be a member of the Lord's body is indeed a privilege. But the privilege of being invited in a special way to join God's people brings with it major responsibilities. The Lord has chosen us to do his work. Our task is to share the good news of Jesus Christ, the way to the Father for all spiritual travelers.

Who is a Catholic?

As we have seen, a Catholic is a Christian who belongs to a faith community which shares Jesus' vision and responds to his presence in our midst. A Catholic loves each member of this community and uses his or her unique talents to contribute to it in a positive way.

A Catholic believes in God, our loving Father. This loving Father has made us brothers and sisters to everyone who has ever lived. Moreover, he has sent us his Son Jesus Christ who won for us our salvation and gave us eternal life.

A Catholic acknowledges the divinity of Jesus Christ, God's Son, our Lord and Savior.

A Catholic believes in the Holy Spirit and the Spirit's powerful presence in the church and in the world. A Catholic accepts and uses the many gifts the Spirit showers on us. It is the Holy Spirit who enables a Catholic to accept Jesus into his or her life.

A Catholic attempts to live in harmony with Jesus' teaching: loving God above all things; loving neighbor as oneself; forgiving enemies; extending special care to the poor, lonely, and the outcast.

A Catholic works for peace and justice, thus helping the Lord promote the spread of his reign on earth as it is in heaven.

A Catholic commemorates the paschal mystery by living a sacramental life. This includes, for example, recognizing a need for forgiveness through the celebration of the sacrament of reconciliation. Moreover, a Catholic cherishes the eucharist as a special sign of God's nourishing love, a way to encounter the living Lord Jesus. A Catholic participates fully in the eucharistic celebration every week.

A Catholic makes time to develop a prayer life because prayer leads to an intimate friendship with the Lord.

A Catholic reveres and reads the Bible, the word of God.

A Catholic acknowledges the role of proper authority in the church, for example, by seeking guidance for moral decisions from the church's official teachers, the pope and the bishops in communion with him.

A Catholic serves others by imitating Jesus who washed the feet of his disciples and commanded us to do the same.

A Catholic proclaims the Lord's gospel, thus publicly acknowledging Jesus Christ and his church. A Catholic is willing to stand up to ridicule and suffering in the service of the gospel truth.

A Catholic is devoted to Mary—the Mother of God and the Mother of the Church—and esteems the saints as models of how to live the Christian life.

A Catholic is fiercely committed to the protection of life, especially in our present age. In a special way, a Catholic defends innocent human life by fighting abortion. Likewise he or she combats euthanasia, assisted suicide, and other contemporary assaults on human life like prejudice, economic policies that exploit the poor, crime and its causes, and the like.

A Catholic is all of the above and much, much more.

But above all else, Catholics belong to Jesus Christ, his church, and to the world to which they come to proclaim in word and deed the good news of our gracious, loving Savior.

Some Traditional Prayers

SIGN OF THE CROSS

In the name of the Father,
and of the Son,
and of the Holy Spirit. Amen.

OUR FATHER

Our Father
who are in heaven,
hallowed be your name.
Your kingdom come;
your will be done be done on earth as it is in
heaven.
Give us this day our daily bread
and forgive us our trespasses
as we forgive those who trespass against us.
And lead us not into temptation,
but deliver us from evil.
For the kingdom, the power and the glory are
yours
now and forever. Amen.

GLORY BE

Glory be to the Father
and to the Son
and to the Holy Spirit,
as it was in the beginning
is now,
and will be forever. Amen.

HAIL MARY

Hail Mary, full of grace,
the Lord is with you.
Blessed are you among women
and blessed is the fruit of your womb, Jesus.
Holy Mary, Mother of God,
pray for us sinners now
and at the hour of our death. Amen.

APOSTLES' CREED

I believe in God, the Father almighty,
creator of heaven and earth.
I believe in Jesus Christ, his only Son, our Lord.
He was conceived by the power of the Holy Spirit
and born of the Virgin Mary.
He suffered under Pontius Pilate, was crucified,
died, and was buried.
He descended to the dead.
On the third day he rose again.
He ascended into heaven, and is seated at the
right hand of the Father.
He will come again to judge the living and the
dead.
I believe in the Holy Spirit,
the holy Catholic church,
the communion of saints,
the forgiveness of sins,
the resurrection of the body,
and life everlasting. Amen.

ACT OF CONTRITION

O my God, I am sorry for my sins with all my heart. In choosing to do wrong and failing to do good, I have sinned against you whom I should love above all things. I firmly intend, with your help, to do penance, to sin no more, and to avoid whatever leads me to sin. Our Savior Jesus Christ suffered and died for us. In his name, my God, have mercy. Amen.

GRACE AT MEALS

Before:

Bless us, O Lord,
and these your gifts,
which we are about to receive from your bounty,
through Christ our Lord. Amen.

After:

We give you thanks, almighty God,
for these and all the gifts
which we have received
from your goodness
through Christ our Lord. Amen.

PRAYER FOR THE FAITHFUL DEPARTED

Eternal rest grant unto them, O Lord.
R: And let perpetual light shine upon them.
May their souls and the souls of all the faithful departed, through the mercy of God, rest in peace.
R: Amen.

PRAYER FOR PEACE
(*attributed to St. Francis of Assisi*)

> Lord, make me an instrument of your peace.
> Where there is hatred, let me sow love;
> where there is injury, pardon;
> where there is doubt, faith;
> where there is despair, hope;
> where there is darkness, light;
> where there is sadness, joy.
> O Divine Master, grant that I may not seek so
>   much to be consoled as to console;
> to be understood, as to understand,
> to be loved, as to love.
> For it is in giving that we receive,
> it is in pardoning that we are pardoned,
> and it is in dying that we are born to eternal life.